Baptist Polity As I See It

Baptist Polity

AS I SEE IT

James L. Sullivan

BROADMAN PRESS
Nashville, Tennessee

© Copyright 1983 • Broadman Press
All rights reserved.

4265-75
ISBN: 0-8054-6575-8

Dewey Decimal Classification: 286
Subject Heading: BAPTISTS / / SOUTHERN BAPTIST CONVENTION
Library of Congress Catalog Card Number: 83-70940

Printed in the United States of America

Dedicated to the memory of
Michael O'Rourke Patterson,
superb professor of Bible at Mississippi College,
who gave me my first concept of the important
relationship between Baptist doctrine and Baptist polity.

To make all men see what is the fellowship of the mystery . . . to the intent that *now* . . . might be known *by the church* the manifold wisdom of God, according to the eternal purpose which he purposed in Christ Jesus our Lord.

(Ephesians 3:9-11, author's italics)

Contents

Foreword

A Baptist pastor in a position of leadership but understanding little about his denomination and its way of doing its work asked, "What is polity, and is it important anyway?" The regrettable thing about his statement was that he was sincere and honest. He meant what he asked, but tragedy lay in the fact that he, in a position of leadership, knew so little about the way his denomination functioned.

The answer to the pastor's question is a positive yes. Polity is of utmost importance. Unless Southern Baptists as a people understand it and how the many facets of the denomination relate to one another, they cannot understand themselves or the work they do together as clearly as they should.

My belief in our denomination is greater by far than it has been since 1926 when I preached my first sermon. There is not one area of Baptist life for which I do not have deep interest and appreciation. There are only four types of organizations existing in the Southern Baptist Convention. They are committees, commissions, institutions, and boards. Interestingly enough, I have served on each one of them in the course of the years. I have served on the Executive Committee of the Southern Baptist Convention, as a commissioner for the Christian Life Commission (when it was the Social Service Commission), as a trustee of The Southern Baptist Theological Seminary (an institution), and as a board member of the Baptist Sunday School Board (trustee) during my pastoral years.

Upon being elected president of the Southern Baptist Convention in 1976, I was required to relate to every branch of denominational life. Too, in that tenure, I was an ex officio member of all boards—Foreign, Home, Sunday School, and Annuity.

Having served as a pastor for over two decades, I have sought to maintain a pastor's point of view. In Baptist associations, I have served in a number of places and states, not only as moderator but in other positions as well. In state Baptist conventions, I have also served on college boards, hospital boards, and state mission boards, even as president of one state Baptist convention. This background has given me an understanding of how local churches, associations, and state conventions function from within.

I have put this book together out of these and other experiences. At first, I contemplated conferring with others to get their suggestions and ideas. On second thought, I vetoed that impulse, preferring rather that the book be wholly mine, influenced by no one. In that way I could candidly express my own viewpoints and opinions and be personally accountable for them. That is the way the book came together as I pulled out of my files materials collected for more than twenty years. In the light of this background, I accept full responsibility for all content. In one sense I am operating here somewhat like a referee at a ballgame, calling the shots as I see them. If anything I have said seems critical, it certainly is not meant to be condemning. Where weaknesses still exist in Baptist polity, or where there is lack of knowledge or disregard for principles under which Southern Baptists are supposed to operate, I have tried to point them out with a hope that future correction can be made. If corrections cannot come forth, perhaps at least improvement can be experienced.

The churches throughout our denomination deserve our best. As we seek to help them be the kind of churches Christ wants them to be, doing their God-assigned tasks to the utmost of their potential, we move on. This is my one overriding objective. It remains my abiding prayer.

James L. Sullivan

Introduction

The germ idea of this book came when I heard a specialist in management say that every system and principle of organization could be illustrated by some fact of physics. Organizational laws and physical laws, like gravity, are fixed by God and have great similarity. Having majored in the field of physics and then moved into management consultant work, this skilled man could identify many similarities between the two. After all, isn't that what Jesus did by his use of parables? His was a truly audiovisual method of instruction. He illustrated the unknown with the familiar. Such an approach helps even an untrained mind to comprehend the deep truths being presented in understandable form.

If such an approach can be made in physics, I asked myself, *why not try using illustrations, graphs, charts, analogies, and any other proven teaching technique to clarify the basic principles of church organization and the method by which denominational polity must be built?* In this way each Baptist might see the principles of polity about which he probably knows too little involved in a living, meaningful way in his own church and denomination. Affairs cannot be handled just any old way within a church or a denomination without creating bigger problems than the ones which have existed before. Had the Wright Brothers not understood the principles of gravity, the design of airplanes would have been impossible for them. Airlines have not tried to change the law of gravity nor repeal it. Rather, they have learned gravity's secrets and tried to accommodate themselves to the nature of God's plan. Thus they fly all over the world.

It is unfortunate, if not tragic, when we violate certain principles written into the plan of God's nature. Doing the right thing in the right way can be almost as important as the deed done. One can conceivably pick coal from the roof or ceiling of a coal mine if he prefers, but it is surely not the easiest way. It is far better to work with the law of gravity in mining coal than to try to resist it. Because the Lord's work in churches and in the denomination is the most important work in the world, God's churches should carry on their work in the most efficient and effective manner available to them. Understanding what to do and how to do it is not easy unless one understands how polity is developed. Southern Baptist polity is essentially our Southern Baptist way of doing things. And the "why" of an action needs to be understood as well as the "what." Then actions can be taken intelligently and meaningfully. When they are, acceptable results usually occur.

Here we're talking about denominational polity—a word seldom used or understood by the average Baptist. But how can a thing seemingly so complex be communicated? This book is an effort to that end. Written in simple, everyday language with understandable illustrations and drawings, it is an attempt to help people comprehend why we *must* do certain things in certain ways.

As a simple local church illustration, consider for a moment a congregational vote which is taken at the end of a service as part of the process of officially receiving people into the membership of that body. Why not let the pastor determine membership himself? Or, would not a committee serve just as well? But the basic cause for doing this is that we have a congregational form of government. This forces us, therefore, to let the congregation express itself in this matter so that we have a knowledge of what the congregation thinks. The vote taken is not literally for the purpose of voting people into the church. Rather, it expresses a congregation's impression about the qualifications of the candidate for membership in the body. If someone is received into the body, under Baptist polity, there must be an expression of willingness on the part of the body.

As Southern Baptists, we are doing things uniquely because Southern Baptists are unique. There is no other denomination like ours. The necessity for fitting change properly into our system can be illustrated mechanically by a carburetor manufactured for an automobile. It works perfectly when placed in that vehicle. But try to fit that same carburetor into an airplane, and it will not work at all. A carburetor must be designed according to the place and way it is to serve and the type of fuel it is to use.

Because Southern Baptists are different from other groups in nature and emphasis as well as procedures, Southern Baptists must, therefore, take steps that are in keeping with their theology and polity, and all actions should be in harmony if there is to be consistency and understanding. Sometimes Southern Baptists are called "narrow Baptists" simply because we cannot do things the same way some other denominations do them. Critics sometimes think we are obstinate and uncooperative if not downright selfish because we do not enter with them into certain methods and activities which they have chosen. What they fail to see is that their established policies by which their work is being accomplished are quite different from the way we do things because of our beliefs and polity.

One of the amazing things of history is how so many right decisions were made by our forefathers who had never read one book on organizational principles. They simply made their choices on the basis of what they thought Jesus would have done in the same situation and in the light of what they thought the Bible taught. They practiced a commonsense, heartfelt procedure and wanted to be fair with every local church and every individual Baptist. They did, however, find it necessary from time-to-time to experiment within rather narrow limitations to discover the best method available to them. Their efforts were wrong on some occasions and the results rather traumatic, as history reveals. Soon, however, they would discover the key and gradually revise their actions until the methods used were both acceptable and efficient to the body. As a result their basic decisions were made in the right way. Our denomination has grown, therefore, and has been blessed almost beyond measure. Making right decisions in polity in the future will become more and more difficult, and more and more necessary. Living in a world that is continuing to expand in population and grow more complex in its international relationships and even in interdenominational relationships, we must stay current in knowing what it is all about.

If this book helps us understand ourselves as Southern Baptists, I will be pleased. The book shows how the denomination functions, and why. Implementing what is learned can help us face the future with courage and optimism and give us motivation. As the right things are done in the right way at the right time, size and complexity cease to be major factors. Our growth can be unlimited.

Right now our polity has a centripetal force rather than a centrifugal one. It pulls us toward each other rather than tending to fling us apart. Oddly enough, some denominations have experienced schism because they have followed a polity which tends to disunite rather than to pull together. Some denominational structures tend to divide rather than to establish confidence. Our polity takes away all threats and appearances of coercion so that each church and person can participate without question marks or reservations.

The principle of voluntarism is fundamental in our denomination and in the development and extension of our local church autonomy principle. By respecting certain principles which God himself has originated and man has identified, churches can cooperate happily, the denomination can stay united, and the work can move forward with speed and happiness. No basic change in the established mode of operations should ever be undertaken without asking what that change would do to Baptist polity. The question of whether the decision will improve the situation or make it more difficult should be asked. Asking why the present procedure was established in the first place is a good practice. Tearing down a fence without asking why it was put there can be a risky process.

In this book I am writing the way I see things, or feel they should be. Readers must take these words in that vein. This route was chosen rather than a deeply-researched historical documentary report which could so easily become enmeshed in minute details, causing readers to become confused rather than informed. Thus communication would bog down. My approach is to present things I have seen or participated in for more than half a century in the Baptist ministry operating actively at the center of things where there were so many eventful happenings. What I have presented are either firsthand observations, or they came out of conversations I had with others who were participants or observers themselves. If others have seen things differently or understood them to be different, let them speak for themselves. Where I have erred in fact, correction will be made gladly. Others may help in clarification where I have failed to express things in understandable fashion.

My most qualifying attribute for writing this book is my ardent love for and support of every area of Southern Baptist life. Each agency, institution, board, state convention, association, and local church has a unique place. So does every individual member of every local church. All of these persons and forces must work together to bring persons to God through Jesus Christ by way of the unique doors open to us as Christian witnesses. Unless Christ is magnified, we have nothing to say. Unless the lost are redeemed and the redeemed are instructed, we have little or nothing to do.

1

Nature and Importance of a Local Church

Most of what Baptists know about Baptists has been learned in local church situations. I know that was true for many years in my own life. It was there that I learned reverence, the Bible's importance and content, and that the church took a vote every time there was a candidate for membership. There, at the appropriate time and in the right manner, I presented myself for membership and was baptized. Even as a lad I sat in on business meetings, listened to pros and cons, came to my own conclusions, and compared them to the church's decisions. In church organizations we studied about Baptist beliefs and practices and why we did certain things certain ways. My first worldwide visions of Christian work came through Sunbeams. My first personal experiences in denominational affairs came when I spoke as a lad to the old Sixth District Baptist Young People's Union in a church I later served as pastor. I witnessed the election and ordination of deacons, heard missionaries speak, learned to lead in prayer and speak publicly. On and on I learned more and more about Baptists from listening and watching.

Many questions, however, remained about Baptists and their way of doing things that could not be answered from observing a local church situation. There was no literature answering questions I was asking. This book seeks to answer questions I had then or came to ask later. I am a more earnest and dedicated Baptist because of what I have learned about us. I hope the same experience will be yours as you delve deeper into Baptist life.

What the church taught me about the Bible, Baptists, the Baptist way of doing things, and a thousand other subjects came with machine-gun speed. Already, seven years before the Cooperative Program was adopted by the Southern

Baptist Convention, that church which I had joined as a lad had manifested its ardent belief in stewardship, missions, and our denomination by voting to send 40 percent of its undesignated gifts to the state executive secretary to be used in support of the various causes of our denomination. Without formal classes in these many areas, I was learning how to be free and yet cooperate with fellow believers in accomplishing tasks too big to do alone. These were my first and most meaningful impressions, my first lessons in denominationalism.

The fellowship and backing of the members of my home church made me feel a part of something far bigger than myself and challenged me to undertake tasks that were way beyond my abilities and years. They seemed to know that it was the constant challenge that would help point me toward the highest heights of my accomplishments, and they never failed to express their faith and prayers in my behalf. I can still hear my pastor saying: "God calls you as you are, but he wants you to become the very best Christian that you are capable of being."

When I finished high school, the Great Depression of the twenties had already hit hard in our hometown. Meeting the sheer necessities of life became most difficult and at times impossible. But my faith never lagged as I faced the future and trusted God each step of the way. Somehow God would provide. And he did. As generous as the offer was, I was not surprised when the superintendent of our Sunday School cornered me after a morning worship service to say, "My wife and I want the privilege of paying your tuition and fees at Mississippi College this coming session if you will permit. If we do that I think that you will be able in some way to care for your room and board." He meant for this to be a gift, but I insisted on repaying him with interest and did. But my church had stepped in again as one of its leaders gave indication of God's leadership in my life, and many others joined to assist. There was no way for my faith to be weak with such demonstrations of daily guidance through this church which will forever be dear to my heart and God's.

I have included this personal experience for two reasons.

One is to point out the importance of a local church doing the best that it knows week-by-week in guiding and training new converts who come into the fellowship of the body. The other is that a thoughtful example on the part of a church in supporting a denomination can lead us into some of our greatest happinesses and opportunities. A church's independence, as it is matched by its interdependence, will give liberal support and affirmation at the times most needed. Just by observation a Baptist can learn much about Southern Baptists and how they do things. In fact, this is the way many of our people have learned Southern Baptist polity, how Southern Baptists do things and why. But it is helpful to go beyond that point of informal learning and apply ourselves now to an analysis of the possible ways to do things and the methods to use as we discover the best way. Because the church of the Lord Jesus is the most important of all of Earth's institutions, it deserves to have the support of its full membership as it seeks better ways of doing its work more effectively.

Before we move on, let each of us look at that local church again where we grew up, and see what it is, where it came from, who constitutes its membership, what it is supposed to do, and what can be its future. A look at the past will help us greatly as we turn our faces to the years ahead.

Let us deal now with some basic questions which will help us to have better understandings and insights concerning what God put the church here to be and do. Then we can understand why it has meant so much to all of us in its daily ministries.

1. What is the church?

Technically, the word *church* refers to those who have been "called out," with the emphasis more on the purpose of being called than what the people have been called from. So, at the outset we see people with a deep sense of mission, as indicated by the name. The definition which many Baptists have learned is that a church is a body of baptized believers, bound together voluntarily by the common bond of love for Jesus Christ working together under God's Holy Spirit to do his work on earth.

The writers of the Bible use many descriptive terms to suggest the nature of the church. It is called "the church of God" (1 Cor. 10:32) or "God's own people" (1 Pet. 2:9, GNB). Jesus alludes to the church as his family (Mark 3:35), or again as "branches," (John 15:1-8), remaining properly related and getting substance from him for life support. More often Paul refers to it as the "body" (Rom. 12:4-5) of which Christ, himself, is the head. This suggests our individual differences yet our fulfillment of the divine purpose as we relate properly to him and to each other just as parts of the body are united so they can function in unison under the controlling head.

Again the church is to be looked upon as "God's field" (1 Cor. 3:9, NASB) planted for the purpose of bearing fruit. It is called the "bride" of Christ (Rev. 21:9), suggesting its nearness to the heart of Christ, and "God's building" (1 Cor. 3:9, NASB) being constructed by his blueprint and for his use.

More than all, it is something that lives, feels, and moves. It is a living organism, a fellowship (1 Cor. 1:9) by which people are blessed. It can rejoice. It can be disappointed. While it cannot of itself redeem a lost sinner, it is a fellowship of the redeemed, thrilling at the thought of God's grace and his eternal love.

Without conflict it is also presented as an organization. It is an organism in which each part is functioning in coordinate relationship with the other parts. It has officers, stated duties, and clear-cut objectives. It has a timetable. It asks reporting from those sent forth from it to do specific duties.

In other words, it is a divine institution with a sacred mission on earth. One is honored and blessed to be a part of such a living body in which there is a blessed ongoing fellowship.

2. Where did it come from?

Jesus answered this question explicitly when he said, "I will build *my* church" (Matt. 16:18, author's italics). It came from him. It has a divine origin and a divine mission. Concepts of the church were first indicated in the Old Testament as relationships of Israel and Jehovah were recalled (Isa.

54:1-10). It was God at work with people on earth to bring about his eternal purpose in the lives of mankind. The idea is also set forth in the deliverance of the children of Israel from bondage as they became "the called out ones," sent on a mission for the Lord.

Trying to pinpoint the exact moment of the church's beginning is not easy. It is like asking, "When does an oak tree begin? Is it an oak tree when it is an acorn, when the root system begins to sprout, when the acorn has become a visible sprout, or when it is a full-grown tree bearing acorns?" Here it is, an oak tree alive and well, but when was the precise moment of its beginning? Some of these things we cannot know precisely. We do know that when Jesus was approached by some of his disciples asking what to do in the case of an argument between two Christians, they were given a method to resolve the problem. Jesus set it forth clearly by asking the one who felt he was wronged to go to the person whom he felt had wronged him, face forward. If a solution could be found between the two of them, well and good. The offender might not even know that he had committed an offense. If this does not work, the one seeking reconciliation should call in a few mutual friends of both parties concerned. Maybe they will suggest an answer agreeable to both. As a last resort, Jesus suggested that they "tell it unto the church" (Matt. 18:15-17). Surely the church was in existence at that time, or Christ would not have given such a specific directive. Likely it took an embryonic form when he called his first disciples to leave their all and follow him and assumed more identifiable shape as his disciples found their places in his service.

The most important thing is not when the church came into being but that it exists, that it is Christ's, and that it has a divine mission as well as a divine founder. Its divine nature is expressed by the type of fellowship and relationship expressed in Ephesians 2:19 where it speaks of a group of "fellow-citizens with the saints, and of the household of God."

I feel that those who date the beginning of the church with Pentecost are incorrect. It was in existence before the Holy

Spirit was sent at Pentecost to dwell continuously in the hearts of believers. This is not to minimize the importance of Pentecost, because that was the date the church was empowered for its divine mission. The Holy Spirit was to be the energizer in the lives of Christian people, a revealer of God's will in the life of the church, and a protector of its people. Without this miraculous gift of the Holy Spirit, the church would have been a workman without hands. Its infilling by the divine spirit was necessary to its future. But the church was set into being before that time.

3. *What is the church to do?*

It becomes clear immediately that the work of the church is aimed in two clear-cut directions, one away from itself to the ends of the earth, the other within itself as it does its assigned task fulfilling responsibilities to those within its membership. Never should one of these directions take the place of the other or crowd out the other. Both directions simultaneously are of utmost importance.

A number of years ago several groups of denominational workers met over a few months with Baptist church members over the entire nation to ask the simple question, "What is the church to do?" There were no commentaries and no prefixed opinions or influences—only Bibles, pencils, and blank note pads. People met and prayed, jotted down notes, and offered personal convictions. Many pages of suggestions were submitted as prayerful inquiry was made of dedicated and capable workers active in the lives of Baptist churches North, South, East, and West.

Represented in the group were people from old churches and new, churches in cities and on the open plains, small ones and large ones. The expressed convictions of these people were later assembled, organized, and expressed in four salient ideas which emerged in crystal clear form. They were namely: worship, proclamation and witness, nurture and education, and ministry. These, they said, in the light of the Bible, constitute the things that the church is to do.

(1) Worship

The church is to communicate with its Creator and to teach its people to do so. They are to seek the divine presence and are to seek to know the divine will. This involves prayer, obedience, and a sense of divine search for life's meaning and God's overall plan for each individual. It was to be engaged in by the group and by individuals who were taught to worship when alone as well as when they were with others.

Worship is perhaps the most distinctive ability mankind possesses and the one thing that most clearly distinguishes mankind from the fishes that swim, the birds that fly, and the beasts that roam. But it is one of mankind's most neglected areas as well as our greatest distinctive. The church is God's effort to give guidance to those who seek to know and do his will.

(2) Proclamation and witness

Mankind was given the ability of speech, as well as something to say. But there has been all too much silence. While there is good news to proclaim and experiences to share, there has been too little witness given by those who know the truth of God. The church is to be active in both proclamation and witness as the truths of heaven are shouted from the housetop in preaching and as individuals share their most intimate personal relationships with others round about.

Only as truth is heard can sinners repent and believe.

(3) Nurture and education

There is to be tender guidance toward the paths of God even in the earliest years of one's life. This involves interpretation and teaching. It is answering life's most often-asked questions. It is dealing with time in the light of eternity. It is blessing others by the verbal sharing of experiences, an ability not given to any other living things God created. The thrust is toward full Christian maturity and full discipleship on the part of every individual believer.

(4) Ministry

The church is to engage in action, stressing doing as well as being. It is to remember that doing God's will is not an afterthought of God. It is one of the fundamental purposes behind the existence of mankind. It is remembering that the first thing Saul of Tarsus asked on the Damascus road was,

"What wilt thou have me *do*?" (Acts 9:6, author's italics). Action became a major role in Paul's discipleship following his Christian conversion. Caring for the needy, feeding the orphans, helping the widows—all these fall within the area of the church's ministry, along with multitudes of other Christian actions expected of all believers. Through the church the Christian's life becomes one of motion as well as emotion.

4. Who constitutes its membership?

One of the main characteristics of a New Testament-like church is that its members are Christian, people who have had similar experiences as in personal encounters they have met face-to-face with Christ and have trusted him for forgiveness and salvation. Without this, there could be no church at all. Christian members must be regenerated, transformed people. Otherwise, they could never understand who Christ is and what he wants them to do on earth. There must have been an experience of "faith" and "trust" in Christ, and a public profession of faith in him, making the church uniquely different from any other organization on earth. Baptism has been accepted as an expression of the new life found in Christ, an audiovisual portrait of an old life laid away and a new life found in the risen Christ.

New Testament churches had high moral and ethical standards for their members and took disciplinary action toward those whose deeds proved an embarrassment to the membership and to the church's reason for being. While there was no perfect church depicted in the Bible, all of them had Christlikeness as their ideal, and their struggles were toward the goal of being like him and pleasing him.

These Christian members voted to make major church decisions in Bible times as they do today.

There are a number of indications that the congregational form of government was used in the early churches. Four of the surest evidences are: (1) Most of Paul's letters were addressed to churches, not just to church leadership, as seen in Romans 1:7. (2) Acts 6:2-3 clearly indicates that "the twelve apostles called the whole group of disciples together and said. . . . choose seven men among you." (3) Acts 10:47

mentions Peter's referral of the matter of accepting certain brethren as prospects for baptism with the words "Can any man forbid water, that these should not be baptized." (4) As Dr. A. T. Robertson pointed out, in Titus 1:5 in which Paul was urging Titus to "appoint church elders in every town," the word "appoint" had as its original meaning "to vote by show of hands," indicating audience participation in the process.

5. *Is the church to act alone or in cooperation with others of similar faith?*

One of the universal concepts of Baptist people is that local churches in the New Testament were autonomous, self-governing, and self-determining. They were certainly individual, in specific locations, such as "the church in Jerusalem," the "church in Antioch," and the "church in Ephesus." In fact, there are relatively few references in the entire Bible suggesting an additional concept, an institutional or universal one. One example is the statement of Jesus, "I will build my church"—stated in the singular but with an institutional meaning. Even here it is likely that he was using the term as you and I would say now, "The *home* is surely facing many troubles today." We've used the singular term with a universal meaning.

For all practical purposes, Baptists must think of local churches as the building blocks of a denomination. They are the units out of which denominations are to be built in the Baptist concept, or there can be no Baptist denomination at all. Each church owns its own property, calls its own pastor, makes its own decisions and lives with them, observes the Lord's Supper, baptizes believers into its membership by standards that it considers the church mandates, ordains pastors and deacons, and many other things that are considered prerogatives of the local church.

At the selfsame time a Baptist church is self-governing it is also interdependent. The Scriptures support these characteristics in several places. Acts 15, for example, clearly shows that all the churches had a common problem. They met together, selected a presiding officer, debated the issues vigorously which were before them, and agreed on the best possible solution available to them. They adjourned and reported to their separate congregations accordingly. Just as mutual problems deserve mutual attention and actions, so do such things as assistance to churches facing financial problems, disasters, or specific human needs, like the poor saints in Jerusalem (Rom. 15) who were assisted as churches pooled their efforts and gifts to alleviate human suffering among their Christian friends in another area. It was common for the churches to entertain pastors of other churches when they were on the road traveling and witnessing in a sort of informal reciprocal arrangement, and they showed Christian love and concern for other believers wherever the churches were located. Never is there any indication that the autonomy of a local church was violated, and always the believers accepted responsibility for their own actions.

No wonder a local church is such an important unit. It is of divine origin, made up of redeemed people, seeking to affirm and bless those in the fellowship, and desiring to give a Christian witness to a waiting world. Multiply this force by some thirty-six thousand, and you can see the dynamic power available for human witness by the people called Southern Baptists. It is an awesome display of almost unlimited potential in the hands of God. Besides, it is motivated by the Spirit of the living God. It is impossible for us to exaggerate what this denomination can do by remaining true to the trust.

The question eternally remains, how can these soul-free believers in their locally autonomous churches combine their efforts and resources in massive worldwide endeavors and still maintain that soul freedom and local church autonomy so dear to them? In the following chapters we will unfold the development whereby this was brought to pass. We will see how Southern Baptist polity developed and became formalized, and we will see how cooperation is made possible without compromise. A study of Southern Baptists reveals the delicate way in which there can be freedom of action and at the same time cooperation in the fulfillment of Christian responsibility in a remarkable way. Checks and balances are properly set into the process for purposes of protection as churches enter with all-out enthusiasm into the endeavors they deem appropriate for coordinated actions without losing any individual freedom or local church autonomy.

2

Forces Which Helped Shape Southern Baptist Life

Having observed the nature and importance of the local church and its meaningful influence on human lives, we still must recognize that it cannot in and by itself do all the Lord's work on earth. In fact, it needs to recognize this significant fact from the beginning. As has already been pointed out, the churches of the New Testament found ways of dealing with mutual problems and obligations by working together, ways by which they could take significant actions together. Nor is there indication that in cooperating any church felt threatened by interchurch endeavors. In other words, they did not feel that compromise was a price which had to be paid for cooperation among churches. To them, cooperation was a strength, not a weakness. Their example stands as a challenge to us.

English Baptists

English Baptists had a profound influence on the American colonies religiously as well as politically. From them came concepts about which the Baptists of America had strong feelings. One was the existence of a state church which sought to force conformity in belief and conduct. The other was the concept of the soul freedom of man which forbade anyone's tampering with a person's beliefs whether it be government or church. Because of these incidents of history, we cannot really understand Southern Baptists unless we begin in England and follow the unfolding developments which helped to bring our denomination into being.

Many of the major denominations like Lutherans and Methodists can pinpoint their beginnings and even name the man who was most responsible for starting them under what they felt was God's leadership. All contemporary Baptists do not agree on the origin of Baptist churches. Some adhere to a Baptist successionism and believe they are able to trace a "trail of blood" from the present back to John the Baptist and Jesus. Others feel that while Baptists have been around for a long time, their actual beginnings are hidden in history somewhere in the dim, dark past. Nevertheless, certain beliefs can be followed from earliest Bible days to the present. Others are convinced that there is adequate evidence to affirm that Baptists grew out of English Separatism in the seventeenth century. The names of John Smyth and Thomas Helwys and the year 1641 are of utmost significance in this documentation. In any case, we cannot recover the kind of early records that would parallel current church rolls, minutes, and other historical data.

It must be remembered that nothing was more dangerous in the era of religious persecution which our forefathers suffered than having a recorded roll of worshipers which could easily be captured by some alert government seeking to put the churches out of business. Some of the early monarchs seemed as efficient in eliminating religious dissenters as they were in facing invading armies. So the rolls and minutes of church meetings were the last things that persecuted Christians wanted. These could be captured and used against them as evidence. Worship was in secret, oftentimes in hiding, and never with public display, or none would have survived this period of intense, organized governmental opposition. So finding written records to prove what we actually believe to be valid points of history is unlikely.

When England got into some of its own political and religious upheavals, Baptists felt they could emerge into the public eye. That they did at the opportune time. It happened this way: About the time of Henry VIII the British kings were in vigorous struggle with the pope at the Vatican. They felt the pope held too much power in their political dominions and that it should be reduced or broken lest the church overshadow the government even to the point of making government impotent. To complicate things all the more, England had laws requiring citizens to hold to the same religious faith as the king. Then as time unfolded and the kings of England were not in religious agreement, the occupants of the throne vacillated back from Catholic to Protestant intermittently. Obviously the people were confused and could not adjust so rapidly so often when they could hardly comprehend what was happening. Not to adopt the faith of the king was a serious matter. First, it was considered heresy, which was bad enough. Worse, it was looked upon as treason because the individual was refusing to follow the official church of the kingdom. The penalties for treason varied from time-to-time but were always serious and oftentimes fatal. The Baptist voice of protest was not the only one heard in these times because the general populace of the land felt the strains of drastic changes in religious beliefs and practices mandated by the crown. Understandable periodic chaos prevailed among the general population in the field of religion.

In this climate, Baptists surfaced and became public. They repudiated the whole idea of religious tolerance and began to cry for religious freedom, wanting no constraints or restraints in matters of worship or a person's desire or ability to worship his Creator. The idea of having to pledge allegiance to the religion of the present monarch was offensive to many people. Baptists were among the loudest voices crying for absolute soul freedom of man in all matters of religion. Such firmness upset many of the governmental leaders all the more—especially the ones accustomed to coercing the populace in matters of the Christian faith and in supporting the church movement of taxing all citizens, including those who disagreed with their positions, for support of the state church. Persecution was a predictable result. This became the experience of many Baptists as they cried out loudly against the influence of the crown and its domination over the spiritual preferences of the people.

Resulting persecution helped thrust many Baptists toward America, along with others who disagreed with the adamant position of the government which had become so offensive to them. Little did the people, who came to America because of Baptist persecution, ever dream of the influence they would have religiously on the American scene. Even now most Southern Baptists have no concept of the almost unspeakable number of influences British Baptists have had on American life. They came to America to get away from the religious persecutions in England, or from the continent which had similar problems, and America seemed to be the best place to flee. So these Baptists began to appear in the American colonies. This meant that Baptists began to champion the cause of religious freedom on these shores, as well as across the sea. Without knowing it, these early Baptists were laying the foundations that would be taken into account for generations to come as spiritual and blood descendants would be fostering the cause of soul freedom which was dear to them. So to understand Southern Baptists, or Baptists in America, one must start with the British Isles to see the background causes and emphases which we adopted and fostered or altered or rejected.

We must also look at that time when the Baptist churches of the British Isles were seeking ways to do things cooperatively. Finding a legitimate base of cooperation was a struggle. All of them believed in the autonomy and interdependence of local churches, and they were constantly alert to keep themselves from being dominated by outside forces. Not only the government but any other influence not internal to themselves was rejected. They wanted the greatest assurance possible that the freedom of the human spirit in worship would not be obliterated through neglect.

At the same time, they were burdened that they were not doing many of the things as Christians and churches which were required of them in New Testament teaching. There were such matters as sending missionaries, caring for the sick, providing for the widows, feeding the orphans, winning the lost, teaching the saved, and equipping the redeemed to reach their highest potential in Christian service. These seemed binding, and at the time each had to be undertaken by a local congregation because they had not found a way of doing such work cooperatively among churches on a nationwide scale. Associations could move in certain areas, but there was a limit because of size and limited resources. Larger Baptist support would be demanded for worldwide operations such as world missions. The question was how these various ministries, made binding on a local church by New Testament teachings, could be carried on by small, poor churches in remote areas if they worked individually and alone. How were they to do such work and at the same time defend the local church autonomy and soul freedom which were so precious to them? How could they set up a denominational structure that could be effective in ministry and at the same time studiously protect the rights of each local congregation?

Anyone familiar with Baptists would expect more than one answer to the questions that were asked about how best to structure an effective cooperative ministry that also protects the local congregation. Two approaches to this problem emerged in English Baptist life. One approach was to choose not to be cooperative in joint ministries. The other approach was to choose to work in a cooperative manner where possible with other Baptists.

Although General Baptists had a more centralized ecclesiology and Particular Baptists magnified the autonomy of the local congregation, it should be indicated that these two approaches to cooperation were not determined necessarily by the doctrinal position of the local congregation. This matter was decided more by individual churches than by theology. Consequently, some General Baptist churches chose to be cooperative; some did not. Likewise, some Particular Baptist churches chose to be cooperative; some did not. A later chapter will emphasize that a close relationship should exist between polity and theology. During this period of early English Baptist history, polity cut across theological boundaries.

The Baptists who chose to be uncooperative assumed a rather isolationist posture. They felt that cooperation might endanger congregational independence and lead to compromise. They chose not to cooperate in joint ventures and simply went their own way. Some see in this approach the roots of the Independent church movement.

The dominant approach among English Baptists was the spirit of cooperation and working together. They worked together when they chose to do so; they did not work together when they chose not to do so. They believed they could work together cooperatively and still maintain and protect local autonomy and soul freedom. Obviously and thankfully, this approach was primary among English Baptists and still prevails as the dominant spirit among Baptists.

Society System

A denominational structure was needed as a vehicle by which Baptists might plan and implement their work together. Any such structure must protect the rights of local congregations and not violate the conscience of any worshiper. They developed a system whereby interested individuals and groups could carry on denominational activities on a broad base with the support of many kindred minds under the aegis of the churches. But such organized movements were not to be over the churches, nor were they ever to force actions or participation. These problems and this effort brought about what is commonly called "the society system" of denominational administration. The society system was based on the voluntary association of those who were interested in a particular concern. A society's purpose was to provide funds and to manage the particular enterprise of interest. Membership was based on financial contributions. It became the basis of much denominational activity in England. It needs to be remembered that it was the British Foreign Mission *Society* which sent William Carey on his first missionary journey. No other system of cooperation which had emerged would protect the meritorious concepts of religious freedom for which they had suffered much and often. A convention-type approach had not been discovered at the time.

Under the society concept they organized societies responsible for publications, educational societies, home mission societies, Bible and tract societies, women's societies, histor-

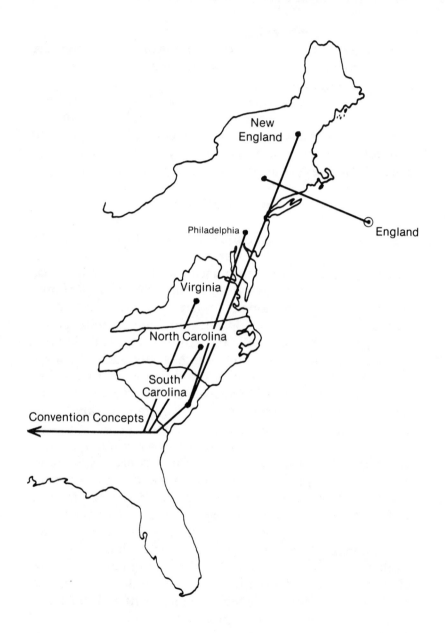

New
England

England

Philadelphia

Virginia

North Carolina

South
Carolina

Convention Concepts

1. British society system of denominational administration transplanted into New England.

2. New Hampshire Baptist Confession of Faith emphasizing autonomy of local church prevailed.

3. Charleston church transplanted to Charleston, South Carolina, from New England.

4. Concept of association came through Philadelphia to Charleston.

5. Concept of soul freedom of man and concept of free church in a free state came mainly from Virginia which suffered most from religious persecution.

6. Shubal Stearns and his Separate Baptists from Sandy Creek, North Carolina added zeal for missions and evangelism as well as informality in worship.

7. Charleston added scholarship, dignity in worship, and good organizational principles.

8. With separation of the Southern Baptist Convention from the Triennial Convention society system in 1845, the flow was westward with Separate Baptists, Regular Baptists, and Particular Baptists.

9. The Northern Baptist Convention (now American Baptist Churches) kept the society system concept, majored on the Philadelphia Confession of Faith with less emphasis on the autonomy of the local church concept, and flowed westward with the population movement.

ical societies, and others. Always these societies were indirectly related to the churches but were not basically an
organizational part of them. They were operated by devout
and dedicated church members and yet were not church-
controlled or -managed. It proved to be the only way they
could move at the time in joint endeavor if they were to
accomplish interchurch cooperation among the Baptists and
do so on a massive base with ardent support in money and
resources from local churches. Obviously no local church
could do all these things alone—even send a foreign missionary alone. By cooperative endeavor, all could have a part
in doing noble things in massive human endeavors when
jointly supported. At the same time, local church autonomy
was assured, and churches could participate fully without
being threatened in any way in their justified concerns for
freedom.

The society concept in due time was to flow westward
across the Atlantic, along with the multitude of capable and
dedicated Baptist leaders who were coming to these shores
to escape unacceptable governmental control over religion in
their native lands. As they came from England, they brought
with them the singing of hymns. This practice was unheard
of until one of the more dynamic Baptist pastors led his
people to have additional music in their worship services
other than the chant of the Psalms which had been predominant until that time. The concept of Baptist district associations came with them to America, and the first associations
on American soil were brought into existence under the
influence of British Baptists. Over the span of the years, the
foundation was laid for the old Triennial Convention (specifically, The General Missionary Convention of the Baptist
Denomination in the United States of America for Foreign
Missions) founded in 1814, the first effort of Baptists on these
shores to organize on the broadest possible basis to help the
churches do the work which they felt should be done as
agents of Christ on earth.

The Triennial Convention, (so named because it met every
third year), emerged out of the society system concept.
Depth of belief led many congregations to rally behind the

missionary movement to send out those who would share
the gospel around the world. Gradually Baptists entered into
other fields in addition to missions and direct missions. Thus
the American Baptist Publication Society, the American Baptist Foreign Mission Society, the Home Mission Society, and
others arose in America somewhat parallel to the way they
had originated in England. There were societies carrying on
women's work, educational work, historical work, and others. Brown University, the University of Chicago, and others
were instituted accordingly, largely by Baptist money and
under Baptist influence. Perhaps it was the only way they
could do things at that time on the American soil similar to
the way it was in England when their society efforts were
first begun. They were noble efforts. Their accomplishments
were many and their influence positive.

Westward Movement

With the passing of time, the society system concepts
which prevailed in the North began to flow westward with
the mobile population as the country was moving and
developing in that direction.

In the South there was the same westward movement with
other influences entering into it. A group of Baptists in New
England under the leadership of their pastor, William
Screven, had moved their church with them as they jour-
neyed to Charleston, South Carolina. Even today it is considered our oldest church, now over three hundred years of
age. They brought with them certain concepts which still
manifest themselves in our Baptist life in a most wholesome
way. Charleston was a privileged city, and the First Baptist
Church of that city became a congregation of privileged
people with highly educated leadership, which gave it a
distinct flavor.

As the movement in organized Baptist life started westward,
however, a group of Baptists in North Carolina under Shubal
Stearns contributed the informality, zeal, and evangelism
which characterized them. And so another element was added
to make a denomination of the people, grass roots in nature,

with mass appeal to the population at every level. Such has helped our growth considerably. Virginia Baptists added the element of religious freedom which they defended vigorously and for which they suffered severely. That concept merged into the emphasis as the movement spread westward; so the Southern Baptist Convention received its name because of its prevailing influence on the South. It is a name which still holds, even though long since considered antiquated. The Southern Baptist Convention has been a national body for quite some years, yet no better name has been found.

The Northern Baptist Convention became the American Baptist Convention, and in time experienced yet another name change. They are known now as American Baptist Churches. They, along with Southern Baptists, find a basis of cooperation in the Baptist World Alliance, but each operates within its own convention according to its traditional lines which developed from their individual histories. So the difference is not doctrinal. Indeed, when Southern Baptists separated in 1845, they made it clear that they did not differ in points of doctrine with Baptists in the North. In an address to the public on May 12, 1845, William B. Johnson, president of the newly organized Southern Baptist Convention, wrote: "Northern and Southern Baptists are still brethren. They differ in no article of faith." Differences which began as cultural became methodological.

Fellowship among Baptist people in the various conventions of North America is wholesome and healthy, but methodology is quite different. Southern Baptists operate on the basis of a convention type of denominational administration which has served well since 1845. Due to a change in 1979, the American Baptist Churches moved from a society type to a churchly type of denominational administration. The American Baptist Churches are now more centralized than the Southern Baptist Convention.

Unity and Diversity

Another wholesome influence on Southern Baptist life which issued from England also needs to be pointed out. On the other side of the Atlantic, the Baptists had few contacts with each other because communications were difficult. Strong leaders had their own individual influences upon their Baptist congregations and groups of Baptists who surrounded them. One group would make one emphasis while another stressed quite another doctrinal concept. In time these doctrinal differences began to assert themselves into heated discussions, even into arguments which led to estrangement between Baptist groups with different emphases. Some became known as General Baptists, others as Separate Baptists or Particular Baptists, or some name which they considered appropriate for themselves. Some were more Calvinistic in doctrine, majoring on the providence of God. Others had been influenced by Armenius and his teachings, placing more emphasis on the freedom of the will. Their basic concepts of individual conversion were essentially the same.

When these Baptists came to the American shores, these detailed differences became less important, began to dissolve, and then merge. Each group made a contribution to Southern Baptist life as they fused into unified efforts in the new land. Under our system of autonomy each could give the desired emphasis, but all were working for the common cause of expanding Christ's witness on the American scene.

How these Baptist groups with different emphases "buried their hatchets" as they crossed the Atlantic was reflected in the First Baptist Church in Charleston, South Carolina, when the church lost its pastor by death. While this church had been related to one Baptist group in England, the members called a pastor who had been aligned with another group of Baptists. The new pastor, Oliver Hart, became one of the most influential Baptists in the building of our nation and in the shaping of Southern Baptist life. He was followed by Richard Furman and Basil Manly, Sr. All emphases were brought together to form a common framework of cooperation. Churches could be different and yet work together cooperatively in magnificent manner.

The phrase "unity and diversity" became the theme and practice of Baptists then, and still remains so. Occasionally, even to this day, a group here and there unduly influenced by some strong leader will begin again to stress some one-emphasis doctrine until it finally will assert itself in the Southern Baptist Convention. Nevertheless, Baptists have understood this and have moved on in unity toward their common objectives. The various groups which had separated in England, each basically having its one predominant emphasis, on these shores became merged into a common fellowship in which their basic individual differences were buried because of the more important work they felt they had to do jointly. *This gave the Southern Baptist Convention a broad base doctrinally with a many-faceted Convention appealing to all types of people of every economic level in every geographical area of the nation.* Each congregation would be responsible to God and to itself and accountable for its decisions and actions. Each church would build its own worship services formally or informally, as it chose. It would provide massive buildings or one-room worship houses as it wished. Churches could even meet under brush arbors if they chose. There were no major compromises of doctrine, but there was a marvelous demonstration of the recognition of religious freedom. Each congregation could feel comfortable within the Southern Baptist framework.

Formation of Southern Baptist Convention

With the passing of years, however, weaknesses began to appear in the society system. As the societies grew larger and new ones were established for different emphases, there was the inevitable overlapping of functions without a centralized, coordinating process. Societies tended to become critical of and competitive with each other. Since societies were self-contained and not necessarily organized at the request of churches, consequently churches did not control societies being operated under the Baptist name. Without a coordinating system to offer directions, societies sought to do what their members wished. These activities might or might not fit the needs and desires of the churches. Nevertheless, the general public often looked upon societies as being accountable to Baptist churches. Although societies had a financial basis of membership, an obvious weakness was that the institutions begun by the society system had no solid, ongoing method of denominational financial support. Persons supporting missions, for example, began to compete with those supporting education. Different societies had annual meetings in different cities at different times. The emphasis of a particular society was stressed, and future plans were made for its specific work. Local churches found themselves in the crossfire of criticism caused by the competitive emphases of various societies. Serious problems began to materialize.

Much of the support of the Triennial Convention came from churches and individuals of the South. Major officers in its operation came from there also. It was the hope of some of the Baptist leaders that the efforts of the societies could be unified so that a donor could support the several causes in which he was interested with a single gift. In this way, it would not be necessary for solicitors for various causes to appear before a local congregation from Sunday to Sunday in order to make appeals for different institutions each time. Furthermore, some in the South felt that Southern areas were being neglected by the mission work of the convention and appealed for more equality. In spite of voices calling for a unified effort of Baptist witness and action, hopes and dreams in this area would not be realized. In 1845 Baptists in the South separated from the Triennial Convention and organized the Southern Baptist Convention.

The controversy which ultimately brought about the final division was the slavery issue. As already indicated, other factors were involved in the separation. However, we cannot be honest with our history and minimize the prominence of the problem of slavery. This question provided the emotional dynamite. It also helped to clarify the weaknesses in the society system which could not stay unified under the pressure of change.

Sectionalism was intensified as people in the South were condemned for ownership of slaves. Some slave owners had fallen heir to situations they disliked. Slaves lived on their plantations, and owners could find no way to emancipate them without witnessing their starvation. While there were those who spoke out against the institution of slavery, there were others who defended slavery and tried to use scriptural grounds for doing so. Thus there were divisions of opinion even in the South. Intensifying emotions, there were those in the South who pointed to the fact that slave ships had been manufactured in New England, and the slaves were brought to the South in those ships and sold at a high price. After their wealth had been secured, then the ship owners and their descendants had become critical of slavery itself. Sectionalism continued to grow larger and more acute, speeding up the day of separation at the Mason-Dixon line.

Complex, many-faceted problems stirred the Baptist leaders of the South to the conviction that the time was right to turn from the society system of denominational administration—a system that had many weaknesses and had become fragmented. When Baptists of the South met in Augusta, Georgia in 1845, they devised a new denominational structure, calling it the Southern Baptist Convention. The charter indicated that the Convention was "created for the purpose of eliciting, combining and directing the energies of the Baptist denomination of christians, for the propagation of the gospel. . . . "

Indeed, a new structure was born. Missions was the foundation, and attention could be given to other areas previously omitted because a way of support could not be found in the society system. Interestingly enough, the words "eliciting, combining and directing" are also included in the charter of the Triennial Convention. In all likelihood, both documents were composed or strongly influenced by the same man, William B. Johnson. It would appear that the purpose of both organizations was similar. How the work was to be achieved was the real question. As will be seen in a later chapter, however, Southern Baptists continued to use the society system methods for a number of years. While the ultimate cause of separation was the slavery issue, it is obvious that other factors, such as denominational structure, were involved.

The Convention, which was made up of messengers (un-instructed representatives sent from churches to find the best Christian ways of doing things together as Baptists) of compatible Baptist churches sharing similar missions and ministries commitments, was not established on a doctrinal basis. It would be established on an action basis with missions being the spearhead of advance in their worldwide spiritual conquest, but all other causes would be included as well. This is why churches are required even now to make tangible financial contributions to Southern Baptist causes as well as to pledge sympathy and support of Southern Baptist Convention causes. A church which would not contribute to the basic causes which had brought the Convention into being would not be happy operating under a Convention system of denominational administration. Therefore, the noncontributing churches were considered ineligible to send messengers to their annual meetings because these meetings had been set to plan actions for the churches in areas where needs could be specifically identified and met on a joint basis. Individual local churches acting alone were considered inadequate.

Conclusion

Baptists today are benefiting by these significant facts of history as all of us serve in God's cause from a broadly-based, missionary-minded foundation with a modified Calvinistic concept. Also, we move on an emphasis on good works as an unavoidable Christian responsibility. The general theme of Southern Baptists is: "Trust, knowing that everything depends on God, but work as though everything depends on you." No such religious body could have emerged without the combination of these divergent forces which God brought together in the earlier days of the shaping of America. The pulsation of progress still goes on. Only God could have controlled the circumstances of the time and brought together this uniqueness of faith and practice which still prevails among us.

3

Least Understood Areas of Southern Baptist Polity

Certain Southern Baptist Convention beliefs and methods are often completely misunderstood. Such misunderstandings produce undue tensions and unnecessary actions on the part of some people and churches. Let me point out some of these erroneous concepts.

1. The churches combine themselves to make up the Baptist associations; the associations are united to form the state Baptist conventions; and the state Baptist conventions when added together make up the Southern Baptist Convention. **Wrong.** Each Baptist body is made up of messengers sent directly to it from the churches. So while associations and state Baptist conventions are closer than the Southern Baptist Convention to the churches geographically, all these organizational groups are equidistant organizationally. Southern Baptist Convention agencies, for example, are just as close to the churches organizationally as units of a district Baptist association are. If our Southern Baptist denomination were constructed according to the prevailing misunderstanding, it would in time likely evolve into a totalitarian system illustrated by a pyramid-type organization—akin to the organization of a corporate structure. Such would be totally unacceptable, and it would transform Southern Baptist congregationalism into Southern Baptist presbyterianism! All churches are at the top level; all other Baptist bodies are at a lower level in the denomination's organizational chart.

2. The Southern Baptist Convention is made up of churches. **Incorrect.** It is made up of messengers from churches. This is to prevent the Convention from unduly influencing the churches but at the selfsame time to provide a situation by which the churches can operate the Convention and its agencies in the way that is best as determined by actions of the messengers from all the churches convened in annual session.

3. *The Southern Baptist Convention and the Southern Baptist denomination are synonymous terms.* **Incorrect.** The Southern Baptist Convention is the body of messengers who meet annually, sent by the participating churches, to lay plans for carrying on their worldwide work on a continuing basis and to provide the means and authorization whereby this is to be done. The term *Southern Baptists* refers to the denomination, which is vastly more than the Convention. In fact, it embraces the Southern Baptist Convention, all the state Baptist conventions, all the district Baptist associations of the nation, and all participating Southern Baptist churches, as well as all individual members of each cooperating church. Indeed, while the Woman's Missionary Union is a most important unit of the denomination, it is not an integral part of the Convention, nor is it subject to Convention actions and directives. Thus, it is referred to as auxiliary to the Southern Baptist Convention.

4. *Baptists send delegates to their annual meetings.* **Not so.** Delegates are called by that name because as such they have been given delegated authority and instructions when they leave for an annual meeting. They go to an annual meeting. They vote the way they are told to vote by the churches and technically can take no other stand. Baptists do not function this way. They send "messengers" from the churches who come together as Christian fellow-believers, committed but uninstructed, seeking to find and do God's will according to their best judgment as each matter of concern is presented to them and after adequate discussion has been heard from the floor. Too, their decisions are not binding on any church, theirs or any other. Reports are carried back as information, and each church relates to Convention actions as it deems best.

5. *The president of the Southern Baptist Convention occupies a position of power.* **Incorrect.** His is an unsalaried office, a position of influence and of wonderful honor. His election reflects the confidence of the messengers attending the Convention. But the Southern Baptist Convention historically

has put forth great effort to see to it that the position of the presidency does not become institutionalized into a position of power. Hence the limit of the president's tenure is two one-year terms. Under the constitution his privileges are also limited. He is to preside over the annual session of the Convention according to *Robert's Rules of Order* and according to an approved agenda adopted by the body. He cannot even extend time for discussion of an issue before the body. It is his responsibility to be completely objective on every matter and totally fair in all rulings. He is to see that all sides of all issues are adequately presented. He is to tap the gavel and announce the body dismissed when all matters of business have been completed and a vote is taken by the body to adjourn. Technically, he has virtually completed his constitutional duties at that point until the next Convention. Many of the multitudinous field engagements accepted by him are his own decisions, not constitutionally required. The limited assigned duties of the Convention president between annual sessions of the Convention are spelled out somewhat in detail. He is to name certain committees, some of which in turn nominate other important committees and boards. This intermediary step is taken for the purpose of preventing the president from exercising undue influence over the body during his tenure or between annual sessions. He is permitted to serve as an ex officio member of the Southern Baptist Convention's Executive Committee and its four boards, for the purpose of being familiar with inside operations of these agencies, and so that he can maintain an overall perspective during his tenure. Otherwise, duties assumed by a Convention president are not constitutionally mandated. In fact, they would come nearer being forbidden by the constitution. The Convention historically has a deeply ingrained fear of placing too much power in any one person or at any one point, whether it be an officer or agency.

At least one president (Pat M. Neff) in my memory did little more during his tenure of two years than to preside over the annual sessions. That responsibility he handled with skill. He named the required committees, and that was it. During his consecutive years of service he accepted no field engagements, nor did he issue any declarations, fearing that it might be interpreted to be a usurpation of power which the Convention never intended for him to assume as president.

6. *The organizational structure of the Southern Baptist Convention is identical to that of a state Baptist convention.* **Incorrect.** All structures of Baptists are different. A local church organizes itself one way, a district Baptist association another, a state Baptist convention (or *general association*) another, and the Southern Baptist Convention still another. Problems occasionally arise when a person who has served well in one Baptist body moves to serve in another Baptist body and operates as though the two positions were identical. This confusion is noticed especially when a person has served well on a Baptist state executive board, and then is elected to the Executive Committee of the Southern Baptist Convention. Here a person moves from one type of structure to another. It needs to be remembered that there is no executive board in the Southern Baptist Convention. As a member of a state executive board, a person would be accustomed to making decisions in all areas between convention meetings. As a member of the Executive Committee, a person would act between Convention meetings only in areas not provided for. Relationships to Convention agencies are therefore utterly different. This difference in Baptist bodies and how they all function requires an in-depth orientation period for every new trustee or board member in every area of the denomination's life. Trustee actions taken must fit the nature of the Baptist body or institution being served.

7. *The Sunday School Board is supported by the Cooperative Program; therefore, it ought to give its curriculum materials to churches making Cooperative Program gifts, or at least ought to sell to them at a discount.* **Incorrect.** The Sunday School Board has never and does not now receive gifts through the Cooperative Program or from other such sources. Therefore, there are no funds available to finance discounts on materials or free distribution of church literature. The Board was set up to produce educational materials and programs to be used by local churches in their inside Bible teaching, membership

training, and worship programs. These are materials for local use in local situations and are financed out of local expense budgets of churches, as are the pastors' salaries, insurance, or utilities. The Board manufactures and sells its materials at a fair market price, financing all of its own assigned programs for assistance to local churches, including service programs. This is understandable and right. If the Sunday School Board did its work with Cooperative Program funds and then sold its materials back to the churches, the churches would be paying twice for their materials, once out of the mission side of the budgets and again out of the local expense side of the local church budgets. The present way is practical and fair toward all. Receiving no appropriations, the Sunday School Board must be an efficient operation to survive and serve.

8. *An institution can be considered to be a Southern Baptist institution if its trustees and teachers are Southern Baptists.* **Incorrect.** Before an institution is a Southern Baptist Convention institution, its charter must be approved by the Convention, its trustees elected by that body, and regular reports made back to the Convention for evaluation and redirection if actions taken are considered improper. Southern Baptist agencies are subject to the will of the Convention. If there were a bank owned and operated entirely by Baptist individuals, would that make it a Southern Baptist bank? Surely not.

9. *An annual session of the Southern Baptist Convention is for the purpose of inspiration, and the program should be tailored to that end.* **Incorrect.** An annual session is a giant annual business meeting of Baptist messengers for the purpose of handling matters of common interest which can be handled in no other way at no other place. While the Convention sermon and occasional addresses are to be inspirational in nature, they are never to crowd out the handling of business matters which constitute the Convention's main reason for being. If the Convention fails in its business responsibilities, too much responsibility is thrown onto Convention boards and their administrative heads, which becomes unfortunate for all concerned. They do not desire or deserve such responsibilities.

10. *Southern Baptist Convention agencies, once established and strong, tend to grow away from the people and assume too much power unto themselves.* **Incorrect.** The churches by their very nature have a way of keeping Southern Baptist Convention agencies close to them and to their basic reasons for being. The charters of agencies authorize privileges within clearly defined limitations. So if an institution were to tend to drift away from its basic purpose, it has the law to pull it back to its main function. Southern Baptists have a double precaution. Agencies cannot change their charters except by Convention approval. This fixes the limits of their authorization or power to act. It defines the area from which they are not to veer. Then Southern Baptist Convention agencies all have rotating boards of trustees, with no one authorized to serve more than two consecutive terms. This keeps fresh ideas coming in from the field so that new input is fed into the planning process. And all trustees are Southern Baptists, members of cooperating Baptist churches. This fixes boards handling matters for the churches with a local interest and viewpoint. Even if all of these fail, there is still the annual session of the Convention where each agency, according to bylaw 28(3), must reserve one-third of its assigned time on the program for questions and answers from the floor. Answers which cannot be immediately given are dealt with as quickly as possible and reported back when facts are available. Every question by every messenger, indeed every church, deserves a courteous consideration and reply.

11. *There is only one right way to do a thing.* **Wrong.** While on moral and ethical issues this may be correct, the principle does not apply to most nonmoral matters. There are usually many good ways of doing something. The quest of the Convention is to find the best possible way with the fewest number of weaknesses, knowing that there is no such thing as a perfect system. Diversity is our way of life. Democratic processes cannot function unless there is diversity, and this ensures the presentation of several viewpoints for consideration. Baptists are diverse in their backgrounds, as well as in their modes of operation. Baptists are different in many ways in different areas, and are different even among themselves

within a local church. This is not a weakness. This is a strength—a major strength. Just because a thing is done in a certain way in one geographical area does not mean that it is incorrect for Baptists in another place to do the same thing differently. Baptists do not believe in religious toleration but in religious freedom. As that freedom is expressed, many good and creative new ways can be discovered and implemented. This keeps the Convention dynamic and vibrant. Experience reveals the wrong, poor, good, and best ways of doing things. Weaknesses can be identified and dealt with. Strengths can be exploited.

12. *The way the Convention controls its institutions is by allocating Cooperative Program funds or by withholding funds from them.* **Wrong.** While funds may be increased or decreased by the Convention, or even withheld entirely, it will not be through any disciplinary action. Cooperative Program funds are for support, not control. Control is through duly elected trustees. Trustees (board members) are the ones in charge as defined by law and under Southern Baptist polity. Therefore, if correction needs to be made in an institution or agency, the best way to accomplish the desired change is through contact with the trustees, not through seeking to adjust Cooperative Program funds given to that institution.

4

Polity:
A Puzzle or a Process?

Polity in its simplest terms is "a system by which a group of people choose to govern themselves, or are governed." It applies to every type of organization, whether governmental or religious. Before a mass of people can work together, someone must assume authority and plan for them, or they must develop a system of their own which defines the basis by which they will relate each to the other under a leader they choose. This principle is true in an Indian tribe, General Motors, the Vatican, or a Baptist church. Not understanding the complexities, it is easy for us to chafe at the details involved in trying to determine what is the will of the majority.

During a visit with Dr. Arthur Flake after his retirement, I asked him, "What was the first program you projected for Sunday School advance in the Southern Baptist Convention?" His answer startled me somewhat when he said, "It was to build evergreen Sunday Schools." This puzzled me because I had never heard of an evergreen Sunday School. When I asked him to explain, he stated that when he first came to the Baptist Sunday School Board, Sunday Schools generally were operated only during the summer months when the roads were dry. His first objective was to help the churches build year-round Bible study programs in the churches. I asked him what his major problem was. Again, I was surprised when he answered, "Baptists were constantly complaining about having too many meetings." They were meeting once to twice a month in part-time churches and were already complaining because too many meetings were required of them.

Almost with a voice of a prophet, Dr. Flake concluded the conversation by saying, "There are only two ways by which a thing can be done. One is to set up a small group and turn everything over to it to handle, which Baptists are never going to do. Or, you can have meetings and plan in detail what you intend to do together."

It needs to be remembered, for example, that Roman Catholic polity is what it is because no one planned for it to be anything else. As a result, their membership has little voice in church governmental affairs. People tend to drift toward a totalitarian, or hierarchical, system unless specific plans are made and actions are taken to prevent it.

It is only by teaching Southern Baptists thoroughly about the basic principles of Southern Baptist polity that we will be able to avoid the risk of our denomination's moving unconsciously in an ever-increasing way toward centralization, or control in the hands of a few. If this sad day ever occurs, it will not only be disruptive; it will be catastrophic for Baptists.

It is relatively easy to understand Catholic polity because it is simple, direct, and unbending. It is built from the top, and policies are handed down which people are to accept and obey. But Baptist polity starts with the grass roots instead of some remote office, and a sound groundwork must be properly laid as Baptists at all levels make their contributions to the fullest of their potential even in planning processes. If we can succeed in fully informing not only the leadership of the Convention, but the rank and file of Baptists throughout the entire Convention, we will be moving toward glorious pages of our history.

People must understand that they cannot practice a polity they do not know and one which is a puzzle to them. This failure to understand is all too prevalent in our denomination at the present time, meaning that the danger is already upon us and will increasingly take its toll as things become larger and more complex unless we are vigorously alert. Religious freedom is dear to our people and must be preserved at all costs in every area at all levels. In that way, the denomination which our forefathers envisioned can surge forward toward its highest potential. The more sophisticated a church organization or denomination becomes, the more it tends to lose the masses, unless it makes constant adjustments to stay closely related to them. Under the name of efficiency or economy, it can move away from its people and produce resentment rather than gaining support. Never should we sacrifice our close relationship to the masses of the people simply to attain more efficient operation. Both are important, but to lose contact with the masses can prove devastating.

When things do work correctly, it is a beautiful thing to watch as worthwhile contributions come together from many sources with input made by many people. The mixing of ideas and convictions together may become somewhat like the ingredients in a cake. All of the ingredients are necessary, but each tends to lose its individual identity when it is stirred into the batter. Therefore, some individuals or groups who have made massive contributions in the planning process sometimes conclude that they have been overlooked because they cannot identify the particular item that they thought they had added as the "batter" was being stirred. Continuous communications are imperative so each element of the planning team can stay informed.

Development of Polity

Unfortunately, *polity* is one of those words seldom used and often misunderstood by Baptists. It sounds abstract and complex. Actually it is far simpler than it sounds. It is built on solid principles that become most practical. It has to do with the development and maintenance of a workable system by which a group of people can relate their endeavors in a way that is satisfactory to all of the participants to achieve the desired goals of everyone involved.

There are some principles of polity that universally apply in government, business, and institutional life as well as churches. There are other principles that apply only to churches, which makes the building of a religious polity quite different from building one used in the secular world. These decisions must take every Baptist group into account and look after the welfare of each participant. Tentative agreements sometimes must be tested until the best way is found. Such acceptable actions are usually looked upon as polity principles which later will be formalized into a constitution or some common agreement like a charter or bylaws.

The method by which the rights of individuals are recognized and protected must be written into the statement with utmost care. Never should a majority group advance itself by trampling relentlessly and without concern on the equal rights of any minority unit or individual within the group. In Baptist life, the word we use is *autonomy*, a term which expresses the right of each individual congregation to own its own building, develop its own program, call its own pastor, and be accountable only to God for its decisions and actions. Being autonomous does not prevent congregations from cooperation, but cooperation is impossible unless certain provisions have been written into controlling documents like constitutions to protect the rights of each individual and the autonomy of each group. This book deals with some of the basic principles which have become the most accepted guidelines in Southern Baptist life, revealing the way we must do our work lest we invite opposition inside our denomination. System is necessary in any series of actions. Unless some system is developed, the investment of time and energy is lost, as well as materials wasted. Chaos can result because even one person can surprisingly upset mutual desires of many others within the group. The unfortunate thing is that when such does occur, the denomination or whatever body it is can end up paying for a tug-of-war, buying the rope for them to tug with and feeding each side more and more vitamins so that they can pull harder against the other. Thus the body pays the cost of both sides of the struggle. This is not only costly and frustrating. It can be destructive.

There are three basic elements in the development of polity for a secular organization, but there are four when it is being determined for a religious body. The three elements that go into the building of polity in a nonreligious organization are tradition, law, and sound organizational principles. All have been proven valid and necessary. The additional element that goes into the development of polity for a religious body is theology. Usually it becomes the most vital factor in the structuring of denominational polity.

Let us look at each of these to see how they affect our own polity as Southern Baptists.

Tradition

As little as we might think of it, we do certain things in certain ways because our forefathers did them that way before us. We never pause to ask why. These traditional practices ought to be the easiest ones for us to discontinue or change. Actually, they are usually the hardest to break or alter. Subconsciously, church members tend to look upon long-practiced principles as fundamentals which should never be revised. This would be a correct point of view if traditions were always soundly based on Scripture. But traditional polity should never be considered sacred unless we relate it to the Bible and find what God has to say on the subject. The problem of tradition is more difficult for the older churches in the more established areas because sometimes they become bound by tradition. Change becomes almost impossible, as they have been frozen into a fixed pattern by having done things a certain way for years. What applies to old churches also can apply to old Sunday School classes. This is one reason we are in the constant process of establishing new ones. The new ones have yet to build their modes of operations and relationships. They can build on good principles without having to forget the old, bad ones. Learning is easier than forgetting. The new organizations of a church just begun do not bind down the body by meaningless traditions which have come to be considered unchangeable.

Let me illustrate this principle by an observation. In my pastoral years I was called to a church which, for decades, had begun every morning service with the singing of the Doxology. It became so commonplace that this unchanging order of service came to be esteemed in itself by many of the members, who would sing through the Doxology by rote in automatic fashion. As pastor, I determined to change the order of service at least to the point of keeping them awake from the beginning, long enough to analyze the words they were singing. On a certain morning I asked the congregation to stand for prayer. The Doxology was not even sung that day. Some of the people went home thinking that I was a theological liberal, or something even worse, because I had not begun the service the way they had traditionally practiced it for decades.

Again, some churches look upon the eleven o'clock hour as a sacred time for holding their morning worship services. This practice began when we were a rural constituency. The eleven o'clock hour gave the maximum amount of travel time from morning milking to evening milking for the farmers who kept their own cattle for their own milk supply. This became traditional to the point that when proposals were made that worship services be held at some other hour, there was sometimes a flareback. Traditions can be firmly fixed and considered binding. They are never easy to change.

Sometimes these traditions become almost ridiculous because people tend to operate in a system without conscious effort once trained to do so. I know a church in which a member offered to give an air-conditioning system to the church and have it installed. The offer was rejected because of the opposition of some of the members who said, "Air-conditioning systems were designed for theaters, nightclubs, and dens of iniquity, and they have no place in the church of the living God." This happened not many decades ago.

While the way of doing things should never be changed for the sake of change, it should be kept updated in areas where improvements are wise and possible. Applications of certain basic principles can often improve situations. Alterations should be made slowly. As binding as tradition is, congregations can eventually be led to improve the way things are done, unless basic violations are made of the way changes should be brought about.

Law

Although we contend for the separation of church and state, we must recognize that we live in a land of law, and churches cannot afford to be lawless. All churches are affected by law whether they wish to be or not. As an illustration, in most states it is impossible for a congregation to own property or buy and sell it. Real estate must be held by an individual or a stated group which is named and identifiable. The law requires that churches name trustees who, in the eyes of the law, actually own the property. If questions arise, the government then can know to whom it can go to handle the problem. This is right, and none of us can argue against the principle. We want our members to be lawful and not rebel against a justifiable legal system. Without fixed laws, anarchy is inevitable. Churches are affected by building codes, fire regulations, traffic patterns, taxation of that part of their property used for commercial purposes, postal regulations, and a host of other things. Law does affect polity.

Fortunately, these legal requirements can be met by a church which controls its own trustee group and, thus, through them controls its property regardless of the way the law considers it. Trustees must be named by every church body of every denomination if it owns its building and land. The name *trustees* will never be found in the Scriptures. Nevertheless, when a church develops its system of operation, it must accept the title to its property and write into its constitution and bylaws the fact of trustee existence.

This section illustrates how laws can and do affect the polity of every individual Baptist church and Baptist body of the nation. We should never seek to develop polity without taking these laws into account. The Southern Baptist Convention has taken proper action and set into its systematic regulation that if the Convention ever orders any of its agencies to do that which is unlawful, the agency is to disregard the instructions of the Convention and abide by the law, reporting such action to the next meeting of the Convention. Later the Convention can take the matter into its own hands to see what the problem is, making whatever adjustment it deems necessary.

Sound Organizational Principles

Again, we are faced with the situation of having to take into account that which is not named directly in the Scriptures. Certain facts are written into nature by God's laws. I refer to the practical organizational principles that are invariably true. They must be practiced lest the organization be weakened or lose its influence. The practical aspects of polity are forced upon us by invisible laws and principles born in the heart of God and written into his act of creation. These cannot be changed and must be taken into account when any basic change in denominational administration is under consideration.

As an illustration, think of a church which is building its own new house of worship. The Bible does not tell it how to build the church building, where to locate it, or even whether we must have a building at all. But when this building is designed, there are some engineering principles which apply regardless of the size or the location of the structure. God in his creative act set into being certain engineering laws when he made the earth. It is our duty to discover, understand, and respect them. There are laws of engineering that apply to a church just as they do to any other building. It is a basic principle that when the roof weighs so much it must be held up by certain wall structures for support. You may try to hold up a heavy roof in the church by a few bamboo poles, thinking because it is a church it should be an exception; but it is foolish to expect God to violate engineering principles he has written in the universe just because it is a church. The roof of a church building will fall in as quickly as that of a department store when these principles are violated.

Churches likewise are bound by organizational principles. The church must understand these and how they work, or it is in for headaches, if not division. Even though it is a church, it must use the same mathematical tables, the same system of counting money, the same method of writing checks, the same way of keeping rolls and recording church budgets and contributions that would be practiced by a certified public accountant. Just because it is a church, it is not granted exemption from these restrictive measures. I know of one pastor who tried to disregard it. Every year in the associational meeting he was cited for having the largest number of additions of any church. When a final study was made, it turned out that he was adding them once when they presented themselves for baptism and adding them again when they were actually baptized into the church. The count was always twice the actual number. He was seeking to disregard the principles of mathematics, thinking that because he was a religious leader these things should not apply to him and his church. There are many practical matters not mentioned in the Scriptures which do affect every church and denomination in existence and influence their way of doing things. The church uses the same sort of typewriter as would be used in an insurance office. It uses the same sort of calculators and adding machines. It is fortunate that the Bible does not go into specific detail in this area of church polity, because updating is constantly needed as we discover more thoroughly the principles which affect us. Even change must be made within certain limitations.

Fortunately, when God said "Go into all of the world" he did not suggest a particular mode of transportation. That can be controlled by the life-style of the people involved and the age in which each witness lives. Flexibility in some areas is possible. Missionaries can go by ox cart, on donkey, in an automobile, or aboard a jet plane, as they wish. It really makes no difference from the Bible's point of view. The vehicle can be updated with the progress of the times without altering the principle. Having discovered the principles that more tightly bind our churches' operations, however, we should practice them without hesitation or complaint. Every pastor knows that when he puts two Sunday School classes in the same room at the same hour under different teachers, he has already created a conflict in his church. Very few church splits just happen. Most of them are caused. A railroad president who puts a locomotive on the tracks at the Atlantic coastline facing westward at the same time he orders an engine put on the same track at the Pacific facing eastward has already created a booming collision even while the trains are still several thousand miles apart. Their collision was not accidental. It was caused by the disregard of basic principles which should have been recognized.

The organizational aspects of polity are unavoidable and

necessary. God wrote certain organizational principles into being when he made us. It is ours to discover and respect them. If we try to disregard or trample them, we are the losers.

The three elements of polity which apply to every type of institution and organization have been presented. There may be others, but these are the most fundamental ones.

There is one other element which applies to churches and religious bodies and is not necessary for business operations, factories, or corporations. That is the theological aspect.

Theology

Theology is basic in Baptist planning because we are a people of the Book. Whatever is in violation of its teachings is and should be rejected forthwith. The theological base for Baptists is perhaps the most valid one we can use. There can never be compromise, if we can be sure what God is saying to us. Once determined, the theological base becomes fixed. It is to be considered unalterable because truth does not change with the passing of the generations. Facts change, but truth is eternal. There is one element, however, that must not be forgotten, and that is that our understanding of what truth is may change from time to time. Our polity must adjust to these newly discovered truths in the Word of God. This is a principle, too, that should never be overlooked or violated.

The Baptist Faith and Message, adopted in 1963, is a wonderful document and sets forth with clarity the prevailing Baptist beliefs among our people the nation over. Doctrine is the backbone around which everything in Baptist life revolves. It is too important to be ignored or downplayed.

At this point it might be well to state that such theologians as Dr. E. Y. Mullins opposed the formulation of a statement of faith in 1925 because he knew by history the tendency of people over a course of time to make a statement of faith into a creed. And creeds have been historically repulsive to our Baptist people. They still are. The difference between a statement of faith and a creed is not in how it is written but in how the statement is used. If it is used as a testimony of mutual beliefs, it is good and right. This is the purpose behind the formulation of the statement as it announces to the world the positions we hold and the interpretations we have made in the light of Bible teaching. But once that same instrument is used for coercion to force others to conform to it, it immediately becomes a handicap instead of a help. It was at this point that Dr. Mullins vigorously opposed formulating a statement of faith for our denomination. It is interesting, though, that when the Convention voted otherwise he was the chairman of the committee that helped formulate the statement of faith in a practical sort of way so that others could know where Baptists stood item by item.

It must be kept crystal clear that the statements of faith approved by the Southern Baptist Convention are not to be misused for purposes of coercion and conformity. These same statements of faith can be helpful organizationally in setting forth the way Southern Baptists are to do things over an extended period of time. This especially is necessary for the agencies and institutions of the Convention so they can operate with consistency and continuity, both of which are necessary in efficient operation. An annual meeting of the Southern Baptist Convention can reverse its positions from one year to the next, but agencies and institutions cannot do so. They are so vast in their operations, and such long-range planning is required of them, that instantaneous reversals in direction are utterly impossible. Institutions by their very nature are unable to reverse themselves immediately, and the larger the institution the more difficult the readjustment. Some vehicles of transportation can make a U-turn with ease, but a freight train of one hundred loaded cars trying to make the same U-turn is destined to end up a pile of debris.

There are two basic theological beliefs which undergird every decision Southern Baptists have made in the field of polity. One is the priesthood of the believer. The second is the autonomy of the local congregation. Because we as Baptists feel that these are clearly set forth in Scriptures, we are forbidden ever to violate the conscience of an individual believer or seek to coerce the members of an individual church. A person's conscience must never be violated. This means that a local church must be structured to protect itself and its members and be cautious lest these two doctrines are violated. At the same time, the local congregation should be cautious lest it violates the conscience of its own members by autocratic or dictatorial methods and leadership inappropriate for a New Testament-like church. Such methods might have been acceptable in the days of Amos and other prophets of the Old Testament, but they have no place in the New Testament setting. Pastors who are dictatorial or autocratic, or churches that allow groups within themselves to assume such roles, will someday pay a high price for this deviation from Baptist heritage.

Again there is the nature of the church as it relates not only to Scripture but to geography. It is looked upon as local. Such a concept forces us into one type of denominational government, with the local church being the most important unit. If the church were looked upon as only universal, we as Baptists would have to readjust our whole approach to all of our work within the Convention. It is well understood, however, that the prevalent, almost universal reference to the church in the New Testament identifies the local congregation in a specific setting.

Putting together the two theological concepts about the importance of the individual believer and the significance of the local congregation, we find ourselves locked into a specific approach in building a denomination. These are important doctrines, scripturally sound, practical in nature, and necessary if there is to be effective functioning as Baptists in a Convention. Never can any agency, anywhere, take the place of a local church, nor should it attempt to do so. The purpose of every Baptist body and agency is to help the church be the church and to accomplish that which they feel God, through his Holy Spirit, is leading them to be and do.

When our denomination took shape, it had to find ways of doing its important work in the light of these basic doctrinal beliefs. Our polity, therefore, was built on the theological concept of the Bible's teaching as to who an individual Christian is and what a local congregation should be.

Development of Southern Baptist Polity

Governments develop their systems of polity in ways utterly different from a church or denomination. They have the power to coerce and enforce, to tax and to unduly influence. They can legislate and regulate, and unless open rebellion is produced, they can eventually win out at least for a while. But even governments with all of their authorities and powers finally come to the place where they must take into account the will of the people whom they govern or face ouster by some future violent revolution. Thus even nations must enact laws that express the desire of the majority whether they wish to do so or not. Even in governments there are precautionary measures set up to see that the rights of individuals are protected. The court systems were originated to see that the lowliest citizen of the land would receive justice in the courtroom.

A denomination like ours must take an entirely different approach because it has no powers to coerce and no laws to enforce. Nor does it want them. The basis by which our denominational system is developed is exactly opposite from government. Other denominations do things differently from Southern Baptists because they see things differently—especially in the field of theology. Because Southern Baptists are different, our approaches and our answers vary oftentimes from the conclusions reached by other religious bodies.

Our Southern Baptist concept is that, organizationally, the church is a local congregation in a local community. So an entirely different method had to be used in developing a workable plan whereby our denomination will function. These churches will be interested in retaining their own local identity and individual control of their own property, pulpit, and affairs as they cooperate. This illustrates how our beliefs predetermine the kind of actions which will be taken by the denomination. Certain emphases may be stressed simultaneously, similar methods used, similar goals set. But where there is a local church emphasis of the "priesthood of the believer" and the "local church" idea is stressed, the body will always insist on a congregational form of government. The wishes of the people should never be overlooked or bypassed.

The usual procedure for Baptists in developing polity is to start with the Bible. We're known as "The People of the Book." The Bible is known as God's revelation to man, giving us acceptable standards by which all human conduct, statements of faith, religious organizations, and Christian beliefs should be tested. In other words, it is our basis for belief and practice. This is so stated in most of the articles of faith drawn up by Baptists everywhere. It is noted that the most complete revelation of God comes in the person of Jesus Christ, who is the center of the Scriptures, the perfect revelation of God to man, a teacher and example, and an adequate supplier of every human need. Organization does not try to disregard that fact. It seeks simply to implement a plan in harmony with God's revelation. It makes mandatory upon people working within the denomination to follow the Spirit of Christ, as well as the letter of the law in everyday practice. It forbids that we adopt a pharisaical attitude, or talk down to people as though they were of little worth. Southern Baptists begin at the point of respect for human personality, a love for God and his Son Jesus Christ, and a respect for the Scriptures which will become our guide in the building of Southern Baptist polity.

A very precise process must be used in relating Bible teaching to Baptist actions. Let us take a look at that unique process which is illustrated by an accompanying chart. First, there must be a knowledge of Bible content. We must know what the Bible says. We must know what it means by what it says. Content and meaning are both imperative. This may require intense concentration and exhaustive study under the Holy Spirit's leadership. We must not only know Christ, but we must also follow the Holy Spirit so that everything done is done under the guidance of the divine Spirit and in a deeply spiritual manner. Every individual participant must be dealt with with respect.

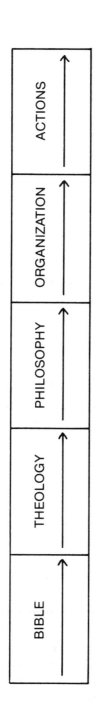

| BIBLE | THEOLOGY | PHILOSOPHY | ORGANIZATION | ACTIONS |

This chart shows the sequential steps of the flow from Bible content to denominational actions. *Bible* content is what the Bible is and says. *Theology* is what the Bible means by what it says systematically. *Philosophy* is the application of Bible teaching to living situations. *Organization* is determined by philosophy, how Bible truths affect the way we relate ourselves to each other. *Actions* are seen by the public. Actions are the steps which find natural expression from the type of organization shaped from Bible content and meaning.

As one masters Bible content and knows the Bible not only to be the Word of God but also knows what it says, he is then ready to begin forming a theology, but not before that time. As the arrow shows in the chart, theology issues directly from Scripture. Theology is the putting together of Bible truths in a systematic way to give us a broad understanding of what the Bible is saying and meaning. From the Scriptures we learn what God is like, who Jesus is, what man's nature is, how sin arose, how salvation is provided, and how a church is to function. Unless theology is based directly upon the Scriptures, it is meaningless. A statement of theology is really putting into different words and systemized fashion what the Bible teaches on specific subjects. The salient thoughts and ideas of God, man, the church, and many other revelations are organized according to particular subjects. It is an organized approach used to see what the Bible has to say on specific issues. It is easy to see how direct Bible teachings will produce theological concepts.

Christian philosophy grows out of theology. It is the method of putting in one's own words how he thinks the Bible teachings find application and daily expression in our lives. Philosophy is the taking of beliefs about Bible content and relating these beliefs to everyday life and works. Philosophy looks at life as a whole. In this approach one determines what makes a Christian redeemed, who followers of Christ are, what they must hold in common with other believers, and what they must do to be pleasing to God. He begins to see, also, that the church is an instrument of God. He is to seek to help the church do what the church is set up to do. Such a statement of philosophy indicates that the Scriptures have come alive and are being applied to the world in the present age, answering the world's questions in today's language and meeting today's acute needs. This statement of philosophy, making practical applications of theology, is a desirable and necessary step. But still we have not reached the point of action. There are other things that must precede the implementation of these concepts.

Organization is the next step. After theology has issued directly from the Bible teaching and philosophy is shaped from the resultant theology formed, there is readiness for the additional step of organization. Organization begins to emerge in a systematic way from philosophy so that work can be done in a cooperative, well-coordinated way. It means that the maximum amount of human good can be done with the least of human efforts. Organization does not come out of thin air. Rather, it issues directly from one's developed philosophy which has been based on theology which has issued from the Scriptures.

While there are voices lifted occasionally against organization itself as being unnecessary and extraneous, it is actually vital and necessary in the work of God that the gospel might be proclaimed in an orderly manner. Certain people seem to be allergic to organizational structure of any kind. They resent and resist it. Instead of condemning organization, however, Jesus practiced it and commended it.

Most people who condemn organization really do not understand its nature. Most of the time they are condemning disorganization without realizing their reversal of thought. Good organization, like good digestion, is something we are unaware of when it is functioning properly. We become conscious of it when it becomes indigestion and begins to create problems for us. We would certainly be in error to try to call it digestion at that point and condemn the whole digestive system.

In its simplest terms, good organization is a tool. It will not move by itself. It does not solve problems by itself. It is like a screwdriver or pair of pliers in the hands of a mechanic. The tools will not do the job, but a mechanic needs the tools if he accomplishes his job well. Organization is a tool in the hands of dedicated Christians who can be effective in helping the churches do a better job.

Good organization works quietly like the law of gravity. If it creaks and makes noises so that you become aware of it, at that point it has become disorganization and needs correction.

Jesus assembled his disciples and sent them out two-by-two. That was organization. He gave them an assignment to do and set certain objectives before them. They carried out his expectation. He asked them to return and report on the results of their visits. This was done. The sending out of the seventy in the Scriptures showed Jesus' belief in and his practice of basic organizational principles. So organization is necessary even if some people are hesitant to recognize its necessity in the work of the kingdom.

Paul likened the church to a human body and cited the various relationships that a human body has with its component parts. Here is the picture of organization at work where each part of the body has a definite function, but all must work together coordinately or the whole body is in pain. After all is said and done, it is the Holy Spirit who motivates and coordinates all Christian efforts. And under his leadership organization can accomplish much. If we trust to organization without the Holy Spirit's leadership, we accomplish nothing.

There is yet one additional step that we must mention briefly, but it is germane to this particular chapter. It deals with that which the public sees—namely, actions. The kind of actions that are seen are determined by the kind of organization that is set up. The average person will not be aware of all the intervening steps that have taken place between Bible content and church actions. They are hardly aware of any of the processes which have gone on before. Leadership is derelict in duty unless it points out that the actions of a church and a church organization or body must be compatible with the Scriptures or they do not help a church perform its God-given functions. Hospitals built by Baptists are actions taken because the Bible calls for compassion and help for the sick and suffering. Children's homes are built because of God's call for us to care for the widows and the orphans. Retirement homes are provided for the aged in their needs as they grow old. Many institutions are set up to carry on actions assisting the churches in the propagation of the gospel. These actions all have their roots in the Scriptures. They were developed by the above tedious step-by-step method of movement from Bible content to church action.

This particular chapter focuses on Southern Baptists with a

view of creating better understanding of ourselves and concerning the "why" of our doing things certain ways. Before we can understand the influence of polity, we must understand its nature and need. In this chapter we have tried to lay a groundwork of understanding of our churches and their people and how cooperation can best be accomplished.

This particular chapter, while focusing on Southern Baptist life, has been general in its presentation. All four steps necessary in the development of religious polity apply to us. The first three—tradition, law and organizational principles—apply generally to all organized bodies. To our Baptist setting must be added the element of theology which to us is of utmost importance. That means that the four basic principles in the development of Southern Baptist polity include the traditional, the legal, the practical, and the theological.

Please know that while we accept this ideal in the development of polity that none of us can fully understand all of the ramifications or put all elements together perfectly continuously. Let me repeat that there is no such thing as a perfect system and that every system has strengths and weaknesses.

It is my studied belief that the Southern Baptist approach in developing its polity has more strengths and fewer weaknesses than any other denominational system available. The way Southern Baptists do things should not be changed without considering all of the elements by which local churches, district associations, state conventions, and the Southern Baptist Convention must find the common ground on which they cooperate. To try to short-circuit these processes is to bring about a slowdown in growth and misunderstandings among the members. The same polity needs to be practiced at every level and in every area to maintain denominational health and growth.

5

Kinds of Denominational Structures

Many factors enter into the development of polity among the various denominations. At times, denominations have been begun by one individual. In these cases, the method of operation might be shaped largely by the temperament or abilities of the organizer. Again, it may be structured so the founder can maintain control of that particular religious body which he has helped bring into existence. Other times polity has been shaped for purposes of efficiency, even patterned after successful governmental or business operations. Or the method of organization and operation might have been chosen which seems most economical or quickest to bring about desired results. Some denominations can be named which really had no harmonized plan; thus their systems are rather complex and conflicting if they have any systems at all. They move without any stated objectives, rolling along aimlessly, letting the waves of change force them to readjust as they meet different circumstances day by day. In such a case it might be difficult to determine what kind of polity they do have and whether there is any particular system by which the denomination functions. When this occurs, the people usually are frustrated and can easily be mobilized by some strong leader who emerges. The results of this development will produce a controlled type of denominational management.

No two denominations are the same, because beliefs and objectives are all different with all groups. The mix of the membership varies from denomination to denomination, and purposes of some church groups can be rather puzzling. Therefore, they must either do things differently by choice or allow them to be done by default.

Even after a denomination has been formed, revisions may

occur as leadership changes, the world scene shifts, or the overall goals of the body are altered. Most of the time denominations seem to adjust, however, within their basic patterns.

History teaches us that an effort to merge denominations into fewer numbers usually results in more denominations coming into existence. Even when the leadership of denominations agree to a merger and have worked out the basis of the merger and the system on which they will operate, there are still problems. The majority may be willing to go along, but there will always be some in each of the merging bodies who refuse to cooperate. They prefer to maintain their traditional system of organization and operation. This frequently happens even with local churches. And where two churches seek to be one, all too often the move ends up with three. This merely stresses the importance of having a sustained mode of operation because people can alter within a particular system, but they frequently will reject a new and different system that someone else seeks to superimpose upon them.

Without trying to be exhaustive, I here present six clearly different types of denominational organizations prevalent today. There may be more. It seems that most major denominations follow one of these six patterns or some variation of them.

1. Informal or Unstructured

This type of denomination can hardly be identified as an organized body. It shuns all types of formal structure. Members are usually a very spiritual people who internalize their religion, waiting to be moved by the Spirit before they do anything even in the local congregation. Then when they do move, it is somewhat on an individual basis or with one person or a small unit leading in the action.

This group oftentimes see the church as two or three worshipers coming together for the experience of fellowship and worship. They prefer everything unstructured. They reject formality and advance planning. Their emphasis is usually on feeling and being more than on doing. Although

•

•   •

•   •

•   •   •

Informal or Unstructured

Represented by small dots which are hardly discernible as organized
bodies, with no formal lines of connection. These people stress informality, spirituality, and humanitarianism. They seem to prefer no formal
organization. This system is inexpensive, unhurried, and has no
central authority. Example: Quakers.

they become activists when they see humanity hurting or
hungering and are willing to organize acts of rescue with
others, they are slow to organize within themselves. They
are especially good when it comes to ministering during
natural catastrophes. They know how to sympathize and
empathize. They serve with intense feeling, deep devotion,
and personal sacrifice.

The Quakers epitomize this group. You can see it personally demonstrated in men like Herbert Hoover, a Quaker,
leading this nation's efforts to save millions of starving
people in Europe at the end of World War I. With him it was a
passion. Without doubt his actions grew out of his early
training in the Quaker background. But to organize as a
denomination and promote denominational activity as
Southern Baptists do would not be acceptable to persons in
this type of denominational structure. They are not institutional or promotional in nature and have no intention of
becoming so.

Many wonderful things can be said about this type of

approach and structure. It is inexpensive. Schedules are unhurried. Fellowships are deep. Christlikeness is stressed and sought, even demonstrated. Nothing pleases them more than to move among people out of deep compassion, helping the blind, feeding the hungry, or caring for the needy.

Weaknesses of such an approach are obvious, also. They have no efficient organization to help maintain sustained action on a broad base when needed. Massive movements are impossible for them. Such a denomination finds it almost impossible to build large mission programs, retirement plans, hospitals, and educational institutions, because of the limitations of the denominational structure.

One of the recognized leaders in a denomination which operates under the informal approach desired to make a tour of Russia. He wanted a trip separate from a tour group so he could see firsthand certain geographical areas an average person on a tour would never be permitted to see. Because he had no denominational structure to back him or aid him in his objective, he made an appeal to the Baptist World Alliance which did plan and set up his itinerary. It secured permissions for his entry behind the Iron Curtain, a trip which he could never have accomplished without the assistance of some large religious body. This noted preacher still says it was the greatest trip of his life, and he is lastingly grateful to Baptists for having arranged something for him which could not be done in the loosely-structured denomination of which he is a part.

This type of approach became especially popular in the 1960s when the cry of many college youths was, "We want creativity, but we do not want structure." These visionary youths failed to realize that the right type of structure can enhance and enlarge creative discovery and expressions. Structure, therefore, can be a friend as well as a foe and should not be rejected simply because of its misuse by some people.

2. Independent and Isolationist

An Independent church is one which seeks to be a denomination within itself. It prefers one central location with massive meetings and highly visible activities. Such a church prefers that all smaller groups around dissolve and become a part of itself, even if they must be bused to one prearranged location far from their homes.

All our Southern Baptist churches are in a very real sense independent, with a little "i," because of local church autonomy and self-determination. The Independent Baptist churches with a capital "I" are quite different. They are more like isolationists but are highly organized within. They stress individualism and individual actions as an organized body. They often become negative and condemning of every other system. In their exclusivism, they become critical even of other Independent churches. Frequently they have major quarrels among themselves.

Instead of supporting our established Southern Baptist schools, they start their own. They do not give through our denomination's mission program. They select and send and supervise people of their own choice. They seem suspicious of others. In fact, they seek to become minidenominations within themselves.

Such an approach has some advantages. An Independent church can move quickly because it is not correlating its efforts with anyone else. Larger denominations naturally move more slowly simply because of size. Independent Baptists seem to grow restless under this sort of situation, preferring to claim all credit for themselves for achievements which have been reached. They build massive Sunday Schools and huge classes for Bible study. They tend to work hard. They minimize classroom discussion or interaction among the members within the classroom as a method of teaching.

Southern Baptists would prefer one hundred smaller churches in a large city ministering in different areas and meeting the diversified needs of the people in ever-changing situations. Independent Baptists seem to prefer to pull all groups into one central location and seek broadly-based media coverage as they do so. The large-classroom situations force them to lecture methods of teaching. Often this is the only approach of instruction open to them. They know that

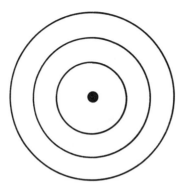

Independent and Isolationist

A local church which chooses to make itself a kind of minidenomination with everything revolving around, issuing from, and accountable to it. Prefers to organize its own colleges, send its own missionaries, and fulfill all denominational functions itself. Usually strong while under a dynamic, charismatic leader but tends toward schism or decrease when this leader passes from the scene. Two variations issue from this form of denominational administration: (1) the Dependent-Independent satellite church which yields its autonomy to the mother church for security and (2) the electronic church which uses mass media to solicit financial support from people without a corresponding personal ministry to them. This system can move quickly, solicits from large audiences over broad areas, and adjusts without consultation with anyone. However, it tends to fall apart when the dynamic and aggressive leaders fade from the scene because of age or death. Such Independent churches may choose to use the name of some major denomination like Independent Methodist, Presbyterian, or Baptist, but they are quite different from these denominations in organization and methodology.

there are many people who will gladly attend who would be reluctant to participate in free discussion. So they appeal to this type of person particularly.

So while the Independent church group has some advantages in speed of operation and individuality of movement, they create other problems for themselves which are inherent in any Independent movement. Southern Baptists, by contrast, seek to be individualistic, but never do they consciously seek to be isolationists.

It is interesting to observe many of the major pastors and leaders in Independent churches which have broken away from the Baptists, Methodists, Presbyterians, or some other denomination. Generally, such leaders are strong personalities and tend to exercise a dominant role of leadership which borders on the autocratic or authoritarian approach. They do not ask. They tell. At times, they even demand. Many times they do not have stated business meetings. The church staff will determine programs and procedures for the people and simply announce what is to be done. One of the interesting observations I have made across the years is how many Independent pastors in their youth engaged in athletics of a particular type. Once in a while you will find one who played football or basketball where his efforts had to be meshed with the efforts and activities of other players. More often they have been boxers or participants in some sports in which they functioned alone. In such sports they would not have to relate to others even in their athletic prowess. Some of their leaders are very aggressive and competitive and prefer the combative situation of an Independent church. This sort of leader may on occasion lose hold on one congregation. If he does, he moves on and starts another which he can control from the beginning.

Independent pastors sometimes hold deed and title to the church buildings so that they cannot be ousted if opposition builds up within the membership against them. While the pastors of Independent churches seem to be secure, this practice proves their insecurity. It shows that they live under threat and are seeking self-protection and declares that they do not have proper confidence in their congregations so as to turn all properties over to them. When as pastors they do not have confidence in their people, the day might come when the congregation will not have confidence in them.

Independent churches seek headlines aggressively and systematically. They frequently do things that average churches would consider unusual or even unethical, such as giving gifts to individuals or groups who enlist the largest group of people in a church activity. They thrive on publicity. They must have it to prosper. An Independent Baptist church can be cited which spent $175,000 for saturation media coverage using radio, TV, and newspapers in its efforts to break the world's record in Sunday School attendance on a single day. They did succeed, but it was impossible for them to teach effectively because all the people could not even get under the roof of the building in which they were meeting. Teaching, therefore, which is the basic purpose of Sunday School, was utterly impossible. The lingering question is, could that $175,000 have been spent more effectively? And was the effort to break a record in numbers the highest objective in the first place?

The basic weakness of this type of approach is that each strong leader will tend to build everything around himself. When the leader passes from the scene his movement or congregation can easily diminish in size and influence. Sometimes it disperses and dies. It becomes somewhat like the proverbial one-man football team. The one man graduates, and everything seems to fall apart with his departure.

Continuity of leadership is necessary in a movement that is to be permanent. Changes, when made, should be gradual and transitional. Independent leaders seem to prefer upheaval and revolutionary approaches. They seem to prefer a situation in flux so that they can referee between adversary groups even within their own congregation. In this way, they forge their own decisions and keep control of the body. In the end, however, inside dissident groups can merge and turn against the leader who has taught them how to make the most of prejudice and conflict.

Under the Independent type of church, two subsidiary movements have appeared which are worth noting but

hardly deserve classification as separate denominational
types. They are the Dependent-Independent churches and
the electronic churches.

The Dependent-Independent church is the one operating
as a satellite of another Independent church, even in some
distant city. It is structured like the mother church and
operates the same way, allowing nothing creative or original
to appear. Some of us can cite one Independent Baptist
church which not only founded a number of satellite
churches, some in distant cities, but enlisted at least a dozen
which once had been cooperating churches in some other
denomination. They were enticed into dependence by theological students from the school of the mother church, who
had offered themselves for assistance in teaching or preaching there. The satellite bodies seem not to care much about
their own self-government. Taking the easy way out, they
follow in the shadow of the larger congregation.

The electronic church may not even be a church in the New
Testament sense. It is built on a television or radio ministry
by a colorful, photogenic, and appealing preacher who
makes constant appeals for funds to support his ministry.
But seldom is an accounting of funds made or a report given.
They influence many people, but there is nothing to join, no
program in which one can actively engage. This type of
situation is so new that valid appraisal of its lasting effectiveness and permanent ministry cannot be made yet.

3. Hierarchical

The totalitarian or hierarchical type of denominational
administration is the most efficient and economical of all. It
has more strengths and also more weaknesses than most of
the other systems. The expense of massive denominational
gatherings for democratic discussions is spared because
decisions are made and announced from a higher level of
denominational leadership. Controls are in the hands of a
few. Decisions are predetermined and superimposed upon
local congregations. Frequently it is as simple as handing
down an order and getting back a report. Quick action is

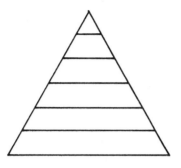

Hierarchical

Structured organizationally like a giant corporation or government. Has several levels of organization and authority. Centralized at the top where most authority is placed. Efficient and economical but tends to ignore rights of individual churches and church members who have little or no voice in overall decision making. General membership virtually disenfranchised. Example: various Catholic bodies.

possible because clearance does not have to come from the masses of the denomination. It is a very efficient and economical system, functioning in a way very similar to the structure of the Roman Empire which stayed in power over seemingly endless generations.

Roman Catholics fall into this category, but they are not the only ones. There are other denominations which are similar in method of operation. In fact it is a well-known approach by several denominations.

While many good things can be said about the hierarchical system of denominational administration, it is not the one approved and adopted by Southern Baptists, for obvious reasons. Baptists feel that in the light of our doctrine of the priesthood of the individual believer, a congregation should be at the top of the organizational ladder, not on the bottom rung. Thus, property should be owned by the local church and leaders selected by that local congregation. Baptists prefer a congregational system of church government which keeps the power and responsibility with the masses of the membership, even though our system is slow and at times burdensome.

While Baptists will defend the right of any group to practice the hierarchical system if it wishes, we prefer to go another way, choosing democratic processes magnifying the worth of each individual and the importance of each local congregation. Our Baptist system also provides for gradual transitions. Our conventions are actually business meetings with masses of people participating in "annual updatings" of our programs and activities. History illustrates that massive changes made in a hierarchical setting almost always require revolutions that produce major upheavals. When they are made, they can bring about divisions similar to the Reformation under Martin Luther's inspiration. Hierarchical systems have difficulty altering their major directions and revising their edicts once they are handed down with finality. While day-to-day decisions can be made more quickly and very smoothly, organizational readjustments and updating are a constant challenge to them and at times appear almost impossible. Even Pope John who called Vatican Council II a few years ago said the conferences were to brush away cobwebs from the church and let in a little fresh air. So, in a system like this, authority flows quickly one way, but massive changes in direction are virtually impossible.

Our Southern Baptist system is in constant readjustment. Every annual session is a readjustment time when redirection is given with the masses of Southern Baptists participating. The difference between the hierarchical system and the democratic system practiced by Southern Baptists can be understood by thinking about the experiences of the scientist who crossed the Pacific in a boat made of matted straw to show how Polynesians could have floated from there to South America to become the first inhabitants generations ago. He tied the bundles of straw together so that they would float and adjust to the waves as they moved by the force of the wind. Caught in a storm, the quaint vessel would creak, but the creakings were adjustments to the waves which came against it with force. In the same storm in which the straw boat survived, regular ships were broken up and sank. Steel cracked under pressure, but the straw boat adjusted to the same waves. It is this principle which baffles newspaper reporters who try to understand and interpret Southern Baptist Conventions in annual session. They listen to the discussions which precede the readjustments. All too often they report that the Convention is coming apart. What they do not understand is that Baptists are binding themselves together in more closely-knit fashion to survive the inevitable storms faced daily by a denomination like ours, the largest Protestant body in North America.

Autocratic systems of denominational administration have their virtues, but they also live with massive problems of their own making. Initiative is usually stifled at lower levels at its point of inception. Creativity often dies aborning.

4. Delegated

A fourth type of denominational system is the one in which a congregation does not wish to be bothered by all the tedious decision-making routines and management necessary to a church or denomination. They do not care for the continuous reporting, vigorous debates, and discussions. Many of them tend to think that these are antispiritual. Inevitably there are affairs which someone has to handle in every church and denomination, if things are to be held together and move forward at all. So churches with a hesitancy to be responsible for the business operations of a church are glad to find someone to whom they can delegate this responsibility. Thus, their polity has taken on a shape rather than a distinctive. They place the responsibilities on the shoulders of people who find the discussions and decisions of a denomination interesting or even fascinating, and the general membership moves on, living with little knowledge of why certain decisions were made or who had the final word.

These denominations may or may not ask for reports to be made to them. Actually they are evading responsibility, abdicating Christian duty, and sacrificing their individual liberty and responsibility as Christians.

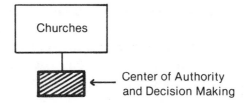

Delegated

Churches whose members dislike being bothered by administrative details and have given these responsibilities to some subsidiary body with power to act. An authoritative group accepts the authority and in essence becomes a board of directors for the body. Members are not bothered by details of administration, but they miss wonderful learning opportunities since they are not involved in the decision-making process and do not know how or why certain decisions are reached. Variations of this delegated form of denominational administration are the Episcopalians and Presbyterians.

The group to whom responsibility for decision making has been delegated may be called by many names, but the management principle is the same. It is in essence a board of management with power to act. It is true that a Baptist church can easily and unconsciously gravitate into this same sort of operation and automatically turn everything over to a management group within the local congregation. Sometimes they do this by passing all business matters to deacons to whom they are willing to relinquish their responsibilities in management and business matters. This sort of abdication of responsibility on the part of some Baptist churches led to the term *Board of Deacons*, when such is foreign to the New Testament nature of deacons. Even though having deacons is scriptural, and they are very necessary in the operation of a church, the Scripture designates them as servants, not as legislators or administrators. The very word *deacon* means "servant." That should be the operating principle under which deacons function.

Perhaps there are some advantages in a delegated system of denominational administration because the congregation does not have to be upset by organization or business meetings or tedious discussions about a sluggish budget or the best use of the dollars that are available. While somebody has to do it, some churches and denominations do not wish to participate in such a process. They select the ones whom they feel can do it best.

Again, this system has virtues, as do the others. Its strength is in the fact that the congregation is rid of the "nuts and bolts" of day-to-day operations in church and denominational matters. They feel that they can, therefore, apply themselves more diligently in the area of the spiritual. This may be possible, but it could be the opposite. The inherent weakness of this approach is that the general membership needs to participate in the planning process or they are not apt to participate in the promotion of their approved activities. Discussions, while at times tedious, are at times necessary in the separation of truth from error. Discussion periods can be highly educational, and many types of people need to make input if proper answers are to be found. Group answers are always safer than individual conclusions. Too, there is always the danger of turning management over to a handful of planners or administrators who may grow away from the people, not fulfilling the desires of the congregation. Once passed on to others, it is hard for a congregation to regain its lost rights. When people participate, they are free to object, to propose alternate routes, even to abstain. But at least they have had opportunity. The spirit of self-improvement is necessary in a local church as well as in the vast operation of a denomination, even in the building of a budget. People are more apt to support a budget they have helped develop than one that is simply announced by some committee in whose actions they have had no part.

Motivation is exceedingly difficult in a delegated system of denominational administration. The congregation tends to unconsciously revert into an observer-type body. Accustomed to observing without participating, they begin to act in the church like persons attending the ball game. They're merely spectators watching others struggle and suffer on the playing field. One thing is interesting to observe in athletics, and that is that the one who does not participate in the game always supposes he knows more than those who do. He feels that his remoteness from the activity makes him an objective observer. Therefore, he becomes critical of every player in the game and what is done under the pressure of activity. A church functions the same way. Participants are the best supporters. When all of the people consider themselves participants in the planning and action processes, it is easy to implement and succeed in excellent plans.

A very important principle was announced by Johann G. Oncken, founder of the Baptist movement of Germany, who made famous the theme, "Every Baptist a missionary." In the Baptist World Alliance you hear this phrase quoted often, and with Baptists overseas, it is profound. While Christianity is personal, it must never be private.

If a denomination is to have strong experienced leaders, there must be a constant ingathering of people with leadership potential. Unless the members participate in the activity of a church, there is no arena in which observers can watch people in actions and evaluate their skills. It is difficult to determine what people can do until they have been seen in action. This is why Southern Baptists have so many denominational leaders and workers who have been seen in action in Sunday Schools, Church Training, music, student work, and missionary activities. Therefore, they have been guided into strong leadership positions in our denomination. When an entire congregation can observe other fellow believers at work, they can evaluate their impact as well as their spirit. This can be very helpful in the selection of dynamic leaders. The church can learn the ones who know how to verbalize well, the ones who are dependable, and the ones who have other leadership qualities necessary to a well-managed religious body.

Churches run by remote control are seldom run well. They

tend to evolve into a division between "us" and "them." This is disruptive. If such a division becomes firmly entrenched it usually gets out-of-hand, and the results are paralyzing.

Of course, all of these actions must be under the leadership of the Almighty or all human efforts fail, regardless of the type of denominational church government practiced.

5. Related

The society system of denominational administration is one in which the churches are related to agencies, institutions, and programs which carry out many activities in their behalf, but the churches choose not to own and operate these entities through a convention and trustees. This method was a spin-off of the British Baptist pattern. You will remember that William Carey was sent out by the British Baptist Missionary Society. The Triennial Convention (1814) used the society method which was continued over a long period by the Northern Baptist Convention which is now known as the American Baptist Churches. As indicated earlier, changes in 1979 moved the American Baptist Churches from a society to a churchly system of denominational administration which is quite centralized.

The primary resource available through which early Baptists might work together was for individuals and/or various groups interested in a special project to align themselves together, dedicate their personal efforts, and pool their financial resources in the promotion of certain denominational functions. These individuals became the sponsors and financial supporters of the causes which later were designated as societies promoting such things as publications, missions, and education. The earliest were primarily for missionary support. Churches appeared to be willing for interested individuals to meet and organize themselves so that the societies they formed could be channels or vehicles through which Christians could combine and coordinate their efforts. In fact, Christians other than Baptists could join a society, which was not exclusively a denominational organization. Since missions was the main objective, a missionary

| Churches | - - - - - → | |

Related

While denominational functions have an informal relationship to the churches, these institutions and agencies are not owned and controlled by the churches. They are free to live or die, be loyal to the purpose of their founders, or veer away if they choose. Operations are according to the society system pioneered by British Baptists. Usually each society majors on one function. Historically each society has been supported by persons primarily interested in one cause more than others. Trustees are frequently self-perpetuating and are free to choose non-Baptists to serve in this capacity. There is little coordination between societies, with each society often meeting in a separate city. The denomination tends to lose its institutions when these institutions choose to stray or change their original purpose or relationship. Financial contributions for societies might come in part from the churches, but they are never accountable to the churches. This was the organizational method of the Triennial Convention which was followed for a number of years by the American Baptist Churches (formerly the American Baptist Convention and before that the Northern Baptist Convention).

society could meet to plan to promote mission projects in agreed areas and solicit financial support from churches, associations, and interested individuals. It takes little imagination to envision a "steady stream" of society members promoting various projects in local churches.

Societies were owned and controlled by the participants who contributed to the cause of a particular society. All supporters were eligible to vote if they contributed. These causes were not church-controlled or owned. With the churches' permission, societies used their relations with the churches and the denomination to the advantage of the societies. However, it must be emphasized that controls were in the hands of the donors who built the budgets, solicited the funds, selected the personnel, and supervised the workers.

The society was the organizational base for all early Baptist mission efforts—in this country and in England. Denominational structures were young and inexperienced. As one might expect, a system was not yet devised by which churches could work together as Southern Baptists do today. In any case, the society system demonstrated that Baptists can work together in common causes. Whether it was William Carey in England or Luther Rice and Adoniram Judson in America, the principle was the same. By united efforts, more can be accomplished than one church can achieve alone.

There are strengths in the society system. Should a need be sensed by the churches, they can encourage interested individuals to undertake the project even if the denomination feels it is premature or even unwarranted for the entire organized body. The project does not have to wait for denominational approval, and the movement can be underway shortly without waiting for necessary actions at many levels as in a vast denomination. When committed individuals become burdened enough for any responsibility that they feel God has made binding upon local churches, they, as individuals, initiate and carry on the necessary organization and promotion to gain financial support and get the movement started.

Some denominations have chosen the society method of operation because they felt it to be speedy and efficient. Churches can have an informal or formal relationship in areas in which they have unusual interests and bypass other denominational activities which to them have lesser importance. The society system is actually a means of designated giving. Yet the churches do not control or own the agencies and institutions under this system. Some who started with this method of operation have shifted from it to seek better ways of coordination and promotion with more equal emphasis on all causes made binding on the local church. At the same time, funds can be divided according to contemporary needs or opportunities.

One of the weaknesses of this system became apparent in Baptist experiences in the United States. As causes began to increase, there was a diversity of opinion and even conflict between those who wanted to support missions and those who wanted to place a major emphasis on education. Southern Baptists are still wrestling with some of the problems caused by institutions which were founded on the society system and which are still related to Southern Baptist life at the present time.

Other weaknesses in the society system become apparent as one studies history. One major weakness of the society system is that it has the experience historically of losing close relationships to many of the institutions it has founded. The denomination and its institutions have grown further and further apart until many of the colleges founded under society systems are hardly recognizable as institutions ever related to a religious body or denomination. The University of Chicago, founded by Baptists with Baptist money, is an illustration of how far an institution under a society system can veer from the original purpose when it gets a self-perpetuating board of trustees. They seem to have a tendency to perpetuate themselves away from any denominational connections or relationships. More unfortunately, some of the institutions have risen up to oppose the very body that brought them into being. Trustees have changed the institution so drastically that it gives little indication of its original purpose. This loss of institutions, or the tendency for them to stray, is the burden of the society system. It is admittedly true that some of the institutions in the Southern Baptist Convention's predominant area of strength have all felt curtailed by the Southern Baptist system of controlled operation. From time to time they have been vocal against efforts to make them accountable to any religious body. Some colleges have been released from a relationship to a state convention in the course of the years because of this insistence.

Another weakness of the society system was that there tended to be a different society for each function of a denominational nature. For example, there was one supporting missions and another supporting education. Still another was set up for publications, another for historical preservation, another for women's work. These societies, while all working in the field of religion, were not coordinated. Each had different leadership. The meetings of the societies were at different times in different places. There was no focal point of coordination or correlation. There was no way to harmonize their efforts or achieve common goals. Soon these societies became competitive and conflicting, and unnecessary difficulties flared.

These obvious weaknesses in the society system caused our Baptist forefathers to look for others ways to work together. As early as the 1817 meeting of the Triennial Convention, efforts were made to establish a more unified approach to denominational cooperation. Perhaps through the influence of Richard Furman, the original purpose of the convention was modified to include home missions. There were other efforts as well. However, by 1826 American Baptists decentralized their denominational operations and chose to use only the society system of denominational administration. This system remained for a long time among Baptists in the North.

Another major step in the search for a new structure was the organization of the Southern Baptist Convention in 1845. When the Southern Baptist Convention was organized, a convention approach was established in order to unify denominational efforts and put denominational causes under the churches through their elected representatives called messengers. Nevertheless, the society system was prominent for a number of years among Southern Baptists. The Southern Baptist Theological Seminary is an example of an institution begun by the society method. However, these early concepts led to the present mode of operation by which the Convention carries on its work.

Although the society system was abandoned in principle when the Southern Baptist Convention was organized, several features of the system were retained until the formation of the Executive Committee in 1917 and the Cooperative Program in 1925. As a matter of fact, the Woman's Missionary Society was founded in 1888 under the society system and still continues to operate under that pattern, though its name has been changed. It finds itself unable to become an integral part of the Convention, though it is a vital part of the denomination and is referred to as "auxiliary" to the Southern Baptist Convention. Organizationally this is necessary because it is impossible for a segment of Baptist life to be controlled by the churches and noncontrolled simultaneously. Under the present system, the Woman's Missionary Union is not accountable to the Convention. It is invited to make reports to the Convention and is informally related, but it is not an organizational part of the Convention itself.

As I see it, one of the items that should be of major concern to Southern Baptists is that certain individuals and groups, desiring a more direct voice in the conduct of Baptist affairs, have established institutions of their own. Several of these schools have experienced considerable success in the last twenty-five years. In reality, the founding of these schools represents a return to the society system in which schools are operated by a means other than through the Convention (or a state convention). You will recall that the society system was rejected by our forefathers in 1845 in favor of a convention system that eventually allowed for control of schools and other institutions through the Convention. We have found this system to be effective and efficient. Indeed, it is highly improbable that a school could be operated at the center of

Southern Baptist life by a society-system approach more adequately than the Convention can do itself with messengers from local churches giving guidance through the trustees.

Should criticism be made of the Southern Baptist Convention by those related to these society-type or independent schools, it needs to be remembered that they are not accountable to the Convention and do not make reports to it—even though Baptist might be in their names. Consequently, the churches through the trustees are not in control of the operations of these independently owned schools. Sometimes reports to their constituents appear to be sketchy and lack the specifics that Convention messengers have come to expect and appreciate. Should the day come when these institutions rise up against their founders and begin to support causes not in accord with the original purposes for which they were created, it will be a repeat of history.

It is unfortunate that some of the independent schools, operated by Baptists but not Convention-owned or controlled, go directly to local Southern Baptist churches to solicit much of their financial support. Most of the time the churches do not realize what is involved in this approach. The Convention has instructed its own institutions that they are not to solicit church budgets for financial support, which the non-Southern Baptist institutions do rather freely. This means that sympathetic treatment is given to institutions which operate in ways counter to the historic Southern Baptist procedure. The incentive structure is upside down in that noncooperating institutions are rewarded with funds from Convention churches. There will come a time when this will create a real problem for Southern Baptists. The churches need to recognize that present-day efforts to re-establish the old society system, whose known weaknesses were long since abandoned by our forefathers, could be unwise.

6. Directed and Balanced

The system preferred and developed by Southern Baptists is the directed and balanced system of denominational administration in which the churches are actually in control of the denomination rather than the denomination being in control of the churches and the balance between associations, state Baptist conventions, and the Southern Baptist Convention is maintained. The will of the body can be ascertained by vote in annual assembly, and those wishes can be carried out through carefully provided procedures. Admittedly it is a slow-moving, expensive, and at times a bunglesome type of denominational government. Its creaking readjustments are heard and oftentimes misunderstood, but it is dynamic and effective in carrying out the wishes of the churches while at the selfsame time protecting the autonomy of each individual congregation and of every church body. Masses of Baptists participate in the planning process. They, therefore, feel themselves participants in the establishment of directions and objectives and give ardently to the causes they support because they have convictions about their inherent merits. Continuity is assured, changes are made gradually, and the system is designed for staggered replacement of trustees over a period of three or four years rather than for an entire board to be changed simultaneously. This requires the necessary passing of time so that the calmer minds can prevail and institutions can have opportunity to reevaluate and take other actions even before final directions are given. There can be a veering of an institution without the trauma of a drastic reversal because of some sudden action of the Convention in an emotional session. Baptist institutions are not like the old handcars on railroads which could make instantaneous reversals of direction. Massive Baptist institutions like the mission boards, the Sunday School Board, the six seminaries, or even the Annuity Board are like fully-loaded locomotives pulling one hundred freight cars at high speed. If instantaneous reversals are undertaken, the result would be a pile of jumbled and disorganized debris. Convention processes require that time for readjustment be provided. This is a planned part of Convention policy. Annual sessions are even held in different cities to keep one section of the country from unduly influencing the body. Two consecutive Conventions are required for changes in the constitution. These are self-protective measures to keep the Convention from overacting or reacting, doing damage to itself by sudden precipitous moves. The Convention seeks to protect itself in many ways, including protection from any tendencies for a hierarchical system ever to evolve in our Baptist life. The Southern Baptist Convention is, of course, a grass roots denomination, and this is the only route we can follow because of the nature of our people, the tradition of our churches, and basic Bible beliefs which are common to us all.

With the feeling that no denomination can be any stronger than the churches which constitute it, there is tremendous emphasis on each local church in every individual community. Individuality is encouraged while cooperation is invited. Even programs are designed so they can be altered to meet individual needs, and the churches are free to innovate. In their innovations, if they make mistakes, the denomination is available to help them find their way out of dilemmas brought upon themselves. The denomination is not structured for the purpose of giving direction to the churches but to make intense study in every area to pass on its experience or the experience and observations of others so that problems can be anticipated before they happen and programs can be evaluated even before they have been launched.

In the next chapter we will examine Southern Baptist life in greater detail. Through discussion and a chart, we will explore the development of Southern Baptist life and will look at the relationships between churches, associations, state conventions, and the Southern Baptist Convention.

6

Developing Organized
Southern Baptist Life

For many years the Baptist struggle to exist in England and in the early years in America was most difficult. Ordinary day-to-day problems were intense enough within themselves. Churches were few and far apart, members were usually limited in financial resources, congregations were lacking in communications, and Baptist institutions had not yet come into being. Add to these conditions the restraining laws of government which always favored the state-sponsored religion, and you get a glimpse of the nature of hardships under which Baptists had to live and serve. To make it still worse, Baptist people generally were looked upon as a disagreeable and dissident people, hard to please and generally uncooperative, if not unpatriotic. This rumor gave them a bad public relations image hard to overcome.

It is understandable that the Baptist congregations were lonely, and at times felt browbeaten by opposition and hungry for fellowship with other believers of their own kind. Too, they must have felt a need for the joining of hands with fellow Baptists for the sake of self-protection as the laws of the land became harder to endure. Survival at times was in question. They all seemed to be suffering alike.

They must have known, also, that the longer they went their separate ways as remote, separated congregations without ongoing communications that the differences among themselves would grow larger and more exaggerated, making future cooperation more difficult if not impossible. Vocabularies expressing their theological beliefs and practices would vary more and more, emphases would differ, and methodology would become increasingly individualistic.

Most of all, they felt an ever-enlarging responsibility for sharing their faith and intensifying their efforts in a worldwide way, fostering missions and ministry. But how could all these widely scattered Baptist congregations accomplish the mighty work they envisioned as a worldwide responsibility laid out for them in New Testament teaching if they continued to act alone and individually? There had to be some vehicle by which they could find a basis of cooperation, whereby they could accomplish many things together which were utterly impossible if they continued their individual actions.

Out of the sense of need and urgency arose the concept of the district Baptist association. The need was widely felt, but how could it be structured so it could help the churches in their needs and hungers for a broader Christian fellowship and at the same time not threaten their autonomy as churches or the soul freedom of their members? The idea of setting up a separate Baptist body, subject and accountable to the churches, seemed to be the only answer. On that basis, they could proceed in faith and with ardent support. But never must an association, once organized, assume the role of lording it over the churches. If it could exist for the purpose of service to the churches by encouraging and promoting fellowship among Baptists, corresponding from church-to-church as the situation warranted, they could see it filling a definite and felt need. It became a matter of utmost importance that they carefully screen the churches feeling similar needs, determining the similarity of their beliefs and the willingness of each congregation to work cooperatively with the others in such a way that no one would try to unduly influence any other congregation.

District Baptist Associations

The earliest Baptist association which can be historically documented was in England in the 1650s. Determining the precise year is difficult. It served the churches well, aided them in their defenses against governmental pressures, and helped them find ways toward growth and ministry. The district associations served so well on the English scene that the idea was brought to America and planted in Philadelphia. Thus, the oldest district Baptist association on the American scene was in that city in 1707, when the associational concept became firmly established under the guiding hand of a British pastor's son, Elias Keach, who was then pastor in Philadelphia. His past experiences, as he accompanied his dynamic father and pastor to associational meetings in England, convinced him of their value, even their necessity, in the new country. From Philadelphia the idea flowed southward and again became fixed as an acceptable mode of Baptist intercooperation. The first district Baptist association in the South was established in Charleston, South Carolina, in 1751.

The scriptural bases for the district association had been found in such passages as Acts 15 and Galatians 2. There were records, also, in the Bible about early benevolent endeavors in the New Testament on a cooperative basis as seen in Acts 11:27-30, 2 Corinthians 8 and 9, Romans 15:15-32, and 1 Corinthians 16:2-6. In these records, no church exercised control over any other body. All felt free to participate voluntarily according to their willingness and abilities.

The basic idea of the district association was essentially the same on each side of the Atlantic with the feeling that there was a scriptural basis for it. A method now had been found whereby Baptists could work together ardently without compromise or the sacrifice of autonomy on the part of any congregation. The associations existed to help the churches be the churches which God wanted them to be and to be servants of those churches in areas where interchurch activities and support were needed and in which movements could be begun and supported. Such causes had been far too large for any local congregation acting on its own. That basic idea still holds, as the Baptist association remains until today a most vital unit in the denominational structure. While it, the state Baptist conventions, and the Southern Baptist Convention are equidistant organizationally from the local church, the association is still in a favored position. It is much closer geographically to the churches and made up of duly-elected messengers sent directly from those churches. This gives the association the advantage of quick action, more personal understanding, and more frequent and meaningful direct contacts. Therefore, the association became and still is a major force in the denomination in interpreting itself and its programs to the churches. Warm fellowships can be experienced among congregations when many of the members are individually known to associational leaders and workers.

That the association is made up of messengers sent directly from the churches is significant. But it also should be noted that in some of the earlier associations reference was occasionally made to an "association of churches" rather than an "association of messengers." The mode of operation, however, has been generally the same. Each church has had its own voice in the associational life, and the association has been a servant of the churches, never a competitor with them.

There is no standard organizational chart developed for use by Baptist associations. They are too varied for that. While most of the early associations in America were formed when transportation routes followed rivers, and hence took their names from them, like the Green River Baptist Association in Kentucky, the prevailing territory of an association now tends to be equivalent to that of a county. Or if Baptist work is still largely undeveloped in an area, the association may cover two or more counties. A county-sized unit is large enough to be effective but small enough to be personal and efficient. So associations which once were shaped according to available modes of transportation now tend to give way to county-sized and -shaped constituencies. The geography of associations generally is kept fluid, and the method is followed which best fits each individual situation.

Some associations are much like they were in the beginning. They are fellowships, attended annually by multitudes of people who come from great distances, bringing their lunches, to hear reports of the churches tabulated over the past year, plan what they can and should do as churches in the year ahead, and experience inspiration from sermons and addresses delivered during the program time. It is a good occasion to meet Baptist leaders from other places and other Baptist bodies and to hear greetings still being sent year-by-year from nearby associations just as they have been doing for centuries. These associations have their elected officers such as moderator and clerk but may or may not have a stated office location or any employed personnel to work with the churches in between the annual meetings of the association. They may have modest budgets and limited meetings, and sporadic assistance might be given as churches request it.

In contrast to the above, some of the associations, especially those in inner cities, are larger and more complex in structure than some state Baptist conventions. They own buildings and employ a host of specialized workers in various fields to serve in many ways, as the churches have requested. They may also own and operate rescue mission stations, sometimes by themselves and sometimes in cooperation with the Home Mission Board. They have educational workers for various age groups, professional counselors to assist pastors with the most difficult cases among their members, and modes of travel that will enable them to meet a crisis situation in short order almost as soon as notification is received.

Most Baptist associations come in between these two contrasted situations just described. While these two types of associations vary greatly in size and budget requirements, they still have the same purpose and relationship to the churches. They are well organized; most of them have one or two employees; a great number of them have stated office locations from which the personnel will function; and the work they do is appreciated by all of the participating churches. Their budgets and size of work are determined by the churches who send designated gifts directly to the association for the support of its work. Associations have and continue to render a fundamental service. Occasionally someone might hear a pessimistic comment such as "The district Baptist association has served its day somewhat like the Baptist academy and should be phased out." Anyone who speaks in that vein is talking in total ignorance either of past history or the present situation. The continuing high

place of the association in the denomination is most significant. It needs encouragement and ardent support on the part
of churches and the people, and its services are indispensable if our Baptist witness is to reach its highest potential in
any given locality.

The existing churches need help and encouragement from
the other churches of the area. Churches in desperate need
can be identified and assistance can be given. Volunteer
workers can be trained and on call when appeals are sent out
for help in the furtherance of any special denominational
emphasis. These needs are current and real. They will not
diminish.

New churches or existing ones desiring fellowship and
participation in local associations are carefully screened by
the association involved to make sure that they will fit into
the Baptist way of doing things, as well as that they hold to
the basic doctrinal beliefs of Baptists. The association is an
appropriate point for any screening of churches done within
the entire denomination because of the proximity of the other
churches making these judgments. Such evaluations are apt
to be more accurate from close range. Nearby churches can
know the churches' attitudes and positions and therefore
state their opinions with more certainty. The church rolls of
state Baptist conventions and the Southern Baptist Convention are usually formed from the rolls of district Baptist
associations, unless someone has given specific information
of the uncooperative spirit of a church and its general
resistance to the denomination and its programs. At that
point, some messenger might register opposition with a
larger Baptist body in the state or Convention, challenging
the seating of messengers from that church which is proving
itself uncooperative.

State Baptist conventions and agencies of the Southern
Baptist Convention show real wisdom when they project
and promote programs in cooperation with the district
Baptist association as a matter of general practice. This keeps
local programs coordinated, and the churches discover easier
ways to plan their own internal activities and organizations.

Across the years, the Home Mission Board and the

Sunday School Board have strongly supported associational work. They have provided funds as well as personnel to keep the associational organizations and activities strong. In places where they have been employed, the directors of missions serving in the associational offices have become key persons in the furtherance of the entire denomination's welfare.

It is necessary to keep in mind that the Baptist association is made up of messengers duly elected and sent by the participating churches. These messengers meet with others with a similar mission, seeking to find better ways by which the Lord's work might be done more effectively and more economically.

Baptist State Conventions

The first state Baptist convention in this country was organized in 1821 in South Carolina, about 170 years after the emergence of the first district Baptist association in England. Basically the same needs which had earlier resulted in the formation of the district associations produced a cry for help on a statewide basis.

Institutions in the South were begun, and they grew. Colleges were organized and were struggling to get proper facilities and financial backing but found their associational base too small for adequate financial support. For the survival and growth of these institutions, a larger constituency was needed to undergird the Baptist work. Children's homes were being begun by Baptist associations, but they soon discovered the same need pressing urgently upon them for more finances from more churches.

Other missionary and benevolent causes were begun. Churches were looking for better ways of doing things. However, their efforts to promote anything but missions under the old Triennial Convention (which was brought into being primarily for missionary support) were frustrated. The promotion of other causes seemed to be handicapped, and the people felt that a better method of overall support must be possible. Too, district associations were becoming more numerous. While they kept in as close contact and communication with each other as they could with their extreme limitations, their work was growing increasingly difficult and more overlapping. They were searching for points of larger contacts and intercommunication with other Baptists. State Baptist papers were for the most part privately owned at the time. What they championed depended largely on the desires and temperament of the editors. These papers made some contributions to the causes but not nearly as much as they do today. State Baptist conventions seemed to be the answer to the dilemma. Why not try and see? South Carolina Baptists were first to pioneer with this project.

How a state Baptist convention could and should be structured was a very legitimate question. To set it up to be a combination of the existing district Baptist associations would be to set a trend toward an organizational structure destined ultimately to become a pyramid-type organization, centralized at the top—a hierarchical structure which Baptists would not long support.

In the earlier days messengers to state Baptist conventions were seated from most of the cooperating groups—for example, churches, associations, missionary societies—who worked together to bring these conventions into existence. Gradually, all of the other representatives were disqualified until only messengers from participating Baptist churches within the state were recognized and seated to handle the state Baptist business matters.

This prevailing concept that developed still is a very fundamental one. It safeguards against the intentional development of a hierarchical church structure. Baptists would have bypassed or abandoned such an approach. Their past experiences had been too painful and too abundant for this type of organization to be acceptable. Churches must continue to be the most important units in any denominational structure. For that reason, the same method was followed in setting up a state Baptist convention that had been followed in organizing local Baptist district associations. Messengers were sent directly from the individual churches.

State Baptist conventions grew and developed twenty-four years before the Southern Baptist Convention was begun. It was learned immediately that they could assist the district Baptist associations just as they gave assistance to the churches, helping each to grow stronger and more completely fulfill its particular mission. Churches and associations were both happy with the assistance of state conventions and the services that could be rendered in their behalf in their missionary, education, and benevolent endeavors.

The state Baptist conventions were structured like the associations, but with more churches and people available to further the major causes which the churches identified as ones on which they needed to center their financial and cooperative endeavors.

State Baptist conventions today engage in many worthwhile causes, in the establishment of new churches and the eliciting of support from older churches for the missionary causes already under way. These state bodies developed promotional methods to which the churches and associations can easily relate and in which they will happily and profitably participate. Today state Baptist conventions are standard and fixed in Southern Baptist life. They operate state Baptist papers, promote missions at home and abroad, and operate schools and colleges, academies and Bible institutions. They operate homes for children and for the aged. They own and operate hospitals, conference centers, camps, and assemblies. They receive and distribute the Cooperative Program Funds given by the churches within the state. They route these funds according to the directives given them by the state convention's messengers, giving a full accounting of all the funds which are verified and announced by regular, published auditing. They assist associations in doing their work. Their influence grows year-by-year through the meritorious way they serve the churches, indeed, the entire denomination.

State Baptist conventions structure themselves in many ways because they vary greatly in age, size, organization, and resources. The prevailing method is for their institutions to operate under boards of trustees who report directly to the full body in the convention's annual sessions. The educational and promotional, stewardship, and missionary work within the state is usually made directly accountable to an executive board and its state executive secretary. Sometimes the state board elects its own executive secretary, and sometimes it is determined that such an individual will be elected by the state convention itself. Nevertheless, departments like Sunday School, Church Training, Music, and others are organized as departments of work under the state executive board. This is utterly different from the approach made in the Southern Baptist Convention, but it can be done effectively within the states because the churches believe it is highly unlikely that there might be a gradual evolvement from a state board into a hierarchical structure within a state Baptist convention. So restraints are not built into charters, constitutions, or bylaws.

The executive boards in some of the states, unlike the Southern Baptist Convention, are declared to be the "convention ad interim," (between meetings), and are authorized to handle anything a state convention would handle in its regular annual session. There is no executive board with such general powers to act within the Southern Baptist Convention. Rather, the Executive Committee is authorized "to act for the Convention ad interim in all matters not otherwise provided for."

The Southern Baptist Convention

Just as there was a felt need for correlation within the states as the district Baptist associations tried to work side-by-side but found their endeavors conflicting and overlapping, so the state Baptist conventions began to feel the need for some systematic way of constant intercommunication and mutual planning to harmonize all their efforts.

Too, there was the feeling of need in other areas such as theological education, the production of printed materials for Bible teaching and church membership training within the churches, and a more systematic way of promoting and directing the ongoing missionary activities that would encompass the globe. The associations and state Baptist conventions proved helpful in their spheres of influence, but they felt they needed help. Therefore, they supported the organization of a larger convention which would encompass the United States where Baptists were strong and could work together on a much broader base with more financial resources. Even the earliest documents of the Southern Baptist Convention spelled out that its area would be the continental United States and its territories. So a national concept existed from the first, although the name used was "Southern Baptist Convention," to pinpoint the area in which Baptist churches predominated and wanted to bring such an organization to pass. The name "Southern Baptist Convention" still prevails, although admittedly it is inadequate and has been from the very first.

Several efforts have been made to find and adopt a more appropriate name. Once a Convention committee was set up to present recommendations. The committee agreed that the title "The American Baptist Convention" was appropriate and should be the new name to be recommended to the next meeting of the Southern Baptist Convention. Announcement was made to this effect by the committee, and plans were laid for such a recommendation to be brought before the next meeting of the Southern Baptist Convention. But the Northern Baptist Convention met first. They proceeded to adopt the proposed name before the Southern Baptist Convention could meet and adopt the committee's recommendation. Thus the name was no longer available to Southern Baptists. Later, the executive secretary of the American Baptist Convention with whom I talked stated their action was taken deliberately, even though there had been no previous committee to study the change. He said it had been done to keep the Southern Baptist Convention from having a name which they felt would be more appropriately theirs. His explanation was, "We have the American Baptist Publication Society, the American Baptist Foreign Mission Society, and other similar titles. If you were to become the American Baptist Convention, there would be endless confusion." So there was no apology on his part for this precipitous action which prevented us from taking the name contemplated.

With other Baptist groups using names like "The National

Baptist Convention," the Southern Baptist Convention has had difficulty finding a name that would be appropriately descriptive. To date, no acceptable name has been placed before the body, although many attempts have been made. Thus the name "Southern Baptist Convention" stands, referring more to organizational concepts and cooperative ministries than to a geographical area, which was the reason for the name at the beginning. It needs to be remembered that the Missouri Lutheran Synod serves a large geographical area and that the Santa Fe Railroad never gets to Santa Fe. So well-known names do not necessarily have to be specific. It is never easy to change a well-known name, especially when it is well liked and easily identifiable. It is more difficult when the institution operates on a national and worldwide basis.

When the Southern Baptist Convention was begun, it followed the same philosophy and doctrines of the state Baptist conventions but involved all the churches and all the organized Baptist bodies in the South wishing to cooperate. For a period of time, it seated messengers not only from local churches but from Baptist associations and societies as well, a practice which was soon phased out. At first, the messengers were called "delegates," but gradually their relationships and nature of work were clarified and the title "messengers" was adopted. That is a name and concept now used exclusively. People continue to come to the Southern Baptist Convention directly from the churches as elected messengers, just as they do in associations and the state Baptist conventions. So the chart of relationships within the Southern Baptist Convention has a similar representation pattern but with a larger geography, more churches, and more people.

The national body was organized to assist and serve the state Baptist conventions in somewhat the same way that they were structured to serve the associations. All were to be servants of the churches, aiding and encouraging them but never seeking to compete with them or to replace them. Nor was the Southern Baptist Convention to replace the state Baptist conventions in their work. If a person thinks state Baptist conventions and district associations are subsidiary to the Southern Baptist Convention, he is in gross error. He misunderstands Southern Baptist polity totally.

In 1845, representatives from churches in several states met in Augusta, Georgia, to organize the Southern Baptist Convention. A brief charter was drawn up in advance which after approval was registered in the state of Georgia, since the first meeting of this convention was held at the First Baptist Church in Augusta in that state. The charter spelled out the nature and purpose of the Southern Baptist Convention and the parties responsible for it. With the approval of the charter, this young convention got started in a very humble way, but the people were full of hope, faith, and commitment. Little did any of them dream that in a span of less than 150 years the Convention they were starting would become the largest non-Catholic religious body in North America.

The Southern Baptist Convention started where it could, with only two boards. Both were mission boards. One was to work within the continental United States and therefore was named "The Domestic and Indian Board," housed in Marion, Alabama. The other was named "The Foreign Mission Board," housed in Richmond, Virginia. It was to establish and serve Southern Baptist churches of the Convention as their missionary agent in areas beyond American shores. While the Bible made no such clear-cut geographical distinction, it was well known that work overseas involved many more complications. A separate board was needed to work with the various governments, languages, and laws. It was felt that a separate board was needed to specialize in these areas and deal intelligently on an international basis with the problems that would be inevitable. Neither board was given priority over the other. Both were considered imperative to the witnessing of a local church beyond its own church field. While theological education and an institution to produce publications were mentioned at the time of the founding of the Convention, funds were considered insufficient. Such causes had to wait for a more appropriate time to begin.

Let me emphasize that it is inaccurate to refer to associations, state conventions, and the Southern Baptist Convention as three levels of Baptist life. It must be remembered that there are no inferior or superior Baptist bodies in the denomination. The chart seeks to point this out as we analyze relationships as they must exist if the denomination is to be healthy. Relationships between associations, states, and the Southern Baptist Convention need to be referred to as areas instead of levels. The word *level* applies only when local churches and denominational units are referred to in their relationships. At that point, the church should be recognized always as the highest level. All denominational units must exist and serve in a way subject to the joint wishes of participating churches.

The church in internal operations has one organizational approach. The association has another. State conventions have yet another. The Southern Baptist Convention follows an entirely different pattern from them all internally, even though each is made up of messengers from local churches. While all were brought into being essentially for aiding local churches in their work, and each bears a similar relationship to the churches, the inner structuring of these various bodies has to be different because the purposes of all the units of organization are individual within themselves. They are not intended to be duplicates but supplementary and complementary in their efforts. Many problems arise if a person serving one area of Baptist life moves over into another and functions with the same attitude in the same way as he did before without recognizing the differences in organizational structure and the specialized organized structure and purposes of these various Baptist bodies.

As the years have passed, each Baptist body has enlarged, enabling it to be of more help in larger spheres of service. The fundamentals of each unit, however, have remained essentially the same.

As Baptist bodies became larger, more restrictive measures were taken by the Convention in annual session to make sure that no large body would dominate the smaller ones and that no one could possibly dominate, or unduly influence, the local churches as they sought to fulfill their own New Testament requirements on Earth. These restrictive measures

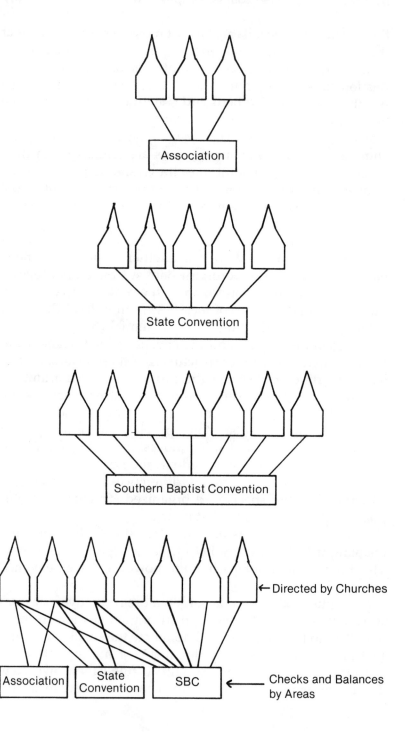

Directed and Balanced

This chart shows several unique features of the Southern Baptist denomination. (1) There are different levels, but the churches are at the top level. The denomination is made subject to them. (2) A number of churches affiliate with a district Baptist association. (3) Those same churches with others added affiliate in the state Baptist convention (or general association), while (4) all are directly affiliated with the Southern Baptist Convention. (5) Associations are the smallest units of organization. (6) State conventions are larger, and (7) the Southern Baptist Convention is largest. However, (8) the Southern Baptist Convention is not over the state conventions or the associations. All are autonomous as are the churches. These three bodies are on the same level organizationally, and all are made up of messengers sent directly by the churches, making them equidistant from the churches organizationally while their territories overlap geographically. There are no inferior or superior Baptist bodies in the Southern Baptist denomination. (9) There are historic built-in checks and balances for the purpose of preserving the freedoms of churches and individual Baptists. (10) Without supreme authority being given to any Baptist body, all work must be done on a volunteer basis through merit. (11) The closest of relationships and confidence must be sought and maintained constantly for the system to function. There is no one with authority or power to coerce in any area or at any level. Each is free in Christ. Each is accountable to God. Direction in the denomination is always determined by the churches but is reflected in the denominational actions they approve and foster. The Southern Baptist system is costly. At times it is slow moving, but this system is considered imperative if the precious heritage of religious freedom is to be preserved.

were written in the constitution and bylaws at the two points where hierarchical organizations could conceivably emerge without anyone's intention or planning. One is at the point of the Convention presidency and the other the Executive Committee of the Southern Baptist Convention. The powers of these have been spelled out in detail and remain specifically limited, though each is essential and of tremendous influence. The authority of action at each of these levels remains restricted.

The powers of the president are now limited primarily by a maximum tenure of only two years. He works through influence and persuasion rather than through granted authority. I have observed that Black Baptists sometimes allow one person to remain as president for many years. In such cases the presidency usually assumes more and more authority without specific authorization from the convention. Southern Baptists were determined that this would not happen in their Convention. Hence, the limitations.

The Executive Committee of the Southern Baptist Convention is the other point at which centralization could occur and gradually evolve into a high level authority unintended by the body. This is why the Convention has an Executive Committee instead of an executive board. Thus matters must be referred constantly to the Convention by recommendation for consideration. The decision level is on the floor of the Convention itself. The Convention has studiously avoided making the Executive Committee into an executive board with automatic powers to act, except in the more routine matters or in entirely new matters which have just arisen. Never can they make policy. While the Executive Committee is a major unit in the Southern Baptist Convention and necessary to the Convention's life and welfare, its authority is specifically and purposefully curtailed. It is responsible for news gathering and dissemination of information, program analysis and recommendation either to or about agencies, and distribution of funds as directed by the Convention in annual session. It has responsibility in a few other routine areas such as preparation and management of the convention hall where annual sessions meet and preparation of daily news bulletins to record happenings on a day-to-day basis. Other such matters are their fixed responsibilities. A committee does not operate like a commission or an institution or a board, but nevertheless it is vitally necessary in the functioning of a democracy such as the Southern Baptist Convention. This can be said with emphasis about the Executive Committee, in spite of its recognized limitations.

Each agency is directly accountable to the Convention. Thus it can be interrogated publicly by any member of that body as any messenger wishes. And the Executive Committee of the Convention is declared to be the Convention ad interim in "matters not otherwise provided for." This means that each agency of the Convention is the Convention ad interim in the area of its own Convention assignment.

Thus the entire Convention moves in mutual trust at every level and must continue to do so. The trust level must be kept high. Unless trust prevails throughout, the entire denomination stagnates.

The Southern Baptist denomination reminds organizational specialists of the bumblebee which scientifically is not supposed to be able to fly. The bumblebee, however, violates every law of aerodynamics and flies about freely, unaware of any limitations. An organizational chart of the Southern Baptist denomination looks like an organizational impossibility. But the miracle is that it works. But only in mutual trust and in common faith under God's leadership can it continue to accomplish that which is seemingly impossible as it effectively works every hour of every day in every part of the world in a systematic way. However, the Convention cannot move forward on organization alone. It must depend on the leading of God to direct every unit of the denomination at every level and in every area as it moves forward in commitment to the high standards set by our forefathers who under God brought our denomination into being.

While we have before us the discussions on the development of the Southern Baptist denomination, along with the illustrating chart, two significant observations should be made at this point so they can be more easily understood.

First, Baptist associations were begun to serve the autonomous churches. State conventions were begun on autonomous bases to serve those associations and autonomous churches while the associations remained autonomous.

Later, the Southern Baptist Convention was organized on an autonomous basis to serve the autonomous state conventions as they assisted autonomous associations set up to serve autonomous churches. Not only is each body autonomous in each area and at every level, but each larger body is to help preserve the autonomy of the smaller bodies to whom they are to relate in the thrust toward denominational objectives. This means that the Southern Baptist Convention, which was organized last, is the largest Baptist body with the greatest responsibility in this regard. The Southern Baptist Convention was not designed to serve the Convention itself or even the Convention agencies. It and its agencies were intended to serve the entire denomination. This makes it mandatory that the operation of Ridgecrest, for example, (which is assigned to the Sunday School Board), is "for the denomination"—not for its own programs or even the programs of the Southern Baptist Convention. This may sound simple, but when we examine its ramifications we find otherwise. Never is advance in one Baptist body to come at the expense of another Baptist body or bodies. All are to cooperate while each is to remain free—with each making its own distinctive contributions.

Second, it is most important that all Baptists know Southern Baptist polity. To fail to understand and respect it can be costly indeed. A perfect example of this is the work of a Convention Survey Committee (Branch Committee) set up in the 1950s with the view of improving coordination in our Baptist work. The chairman of the committee regretfully admitted after the work was done that he and his committee had never paused to distinguish the organizational difference between the Convention and the denomination. As a result the efforts to correlate the work of Convention agencies tended to "un-correlate" the work in the denomination, and the whole planning process was reversed from its historic procedure. State conventions and Baptist associations no longer were involved in the early stages of planning.

Therefore, they felt shut out and were requested to promote a "handed down" program developed without their assistance. As a result, communications between the Southern Baptist Convention organization and the corresponding state and associational organizations bogged down almost entirely. Upheaval resulted among the agencies and church organizations. This contributed to a slowing in our growth rate in nearly every area of Baptist life for a decade, including baptisms. While some corrections have been made, the basic problem still exists. It illustrates that overall denominational problems cannot be solved entirely by Convention-wide committees.

7

Structured
for Massive Ministry

When a mass of Christian people work together in gigantic worldwide endeavors, they must have a clear and systematic method by which they work. Baptist polity gives guidance in the development of that system.

To understand the Southern Baptist Convention, we must look at it from at least two viewpoints. One is what happens when the Convention is in annual session. The other is how it does its work between those annual meetings. In a subsequent chapter we will mentally attend the Southern Baptist Convention in its official annual session to get a glimpse of what happens at that time. In this chapter we will deal with how the Convention carries on its worldwide work on a continuous basis in an efficient and effective manner. It takes twenty-five separate boards, agencies, and institutions to do the work assigned to it.

A look at the chart in this chapter will show that there are four types of approaches set up to handle the diversified, continuing assignments given the Southern Baptist Convention by messengers to the Convention. These are committees, commissions, institutions, and boards. All are important. All are different. Some are well known. Others are hardly known. A few may be generally unknown to most Baptists. Such does not indicate the importance or unimportance of any agency; it only reflects its visibility. All are important. Each has its specific place.

I want to emphasize that the arrangement of this chart does not indicate that any one body is more important or has more authority than any other body. I have used this arrangement to show function and action. Those agencies in the vertical column relate to function; those in the horizontal line relate to action. Let me explain.

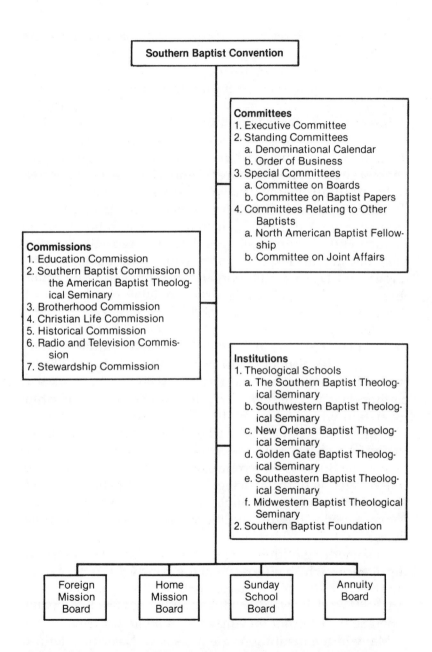

Southern Baptist Convention

Committees
1. Executive Committee
2. Standing Committees
   a. Denominational Calendar
   b. Order of Business
3. Special Committees
   a. Committee on Boards
   b. Committee on Baptist Papers
4. Committees Relating to Other Baptists
   a. North American Baptist Fellowship
   b. Committee on Joint Affairs

Commissions
1. Education Commission
2. Southern Baptist Commission on the American Baptist Theological Seminary
3. Brotherhood Commission
4. Christian Life Commission
5. Historical Commission
6. Radio and Television Commission
7. Stewardship Commission

Institutions
1. Theological Schools
   a. The Southern Baptist Theological Seminary
   b. Southwestern Baptist Theological Seminary
   c. New Orleans Baptist Theological Seminary
   d. Golden Gate Baptist Theological Seminary
   e. Southeastern Baptist Theological Seminary
   f. Midwestern Baptist Theological Seminary
2. Southern Baptist Foundation

| Foreign Mission Board | Home Mission Board | Sunday School Board | Annuity Board |

The Committee on Committees is an ad hoc committee named by the president to nominate members on the Committee on Boards. The Committees named in this chart are the ones elected by the Convention.

People who are active in vast organizational enterprises are familiar with line and staff relationships. They are quite different, even though both are directed toward the same ultimate objectives, and both are necessary. These relationships exist both within agencies and in interagency relations. Primarily staff deals with functions, and line deals with actions. Their work is intermeshed almost in the way the two threads in a sewing machine make stitches. Together they make a strong bond to assure that no major area is neglected.

Let me illustrate the principle by looking at a local church. If it is fully functioning, it has at least two organizations—a Sunday School and a Church Training organization made up of men and women of all ages. Each is a separate organization dealing in a specific area with continuous, ongoing programs. These are line organizations majoring on action. Evangelism, by contrast, is a staff function which relates to both of these organizations and helps each keep in mind constantly this most important function which gives meaning to all that is done in Sunday School and Church Training.

The Sunday School Board provides another good illustration. There are editors and their co-workers who work with authors to prepare copy for print. There is the publishing operation which takes the typed manuscript and produces the finished product. Still others ship the materials as ordered. These are line operations majoring on actions. But inside the Board is an accounting department which handles the budgeting and financing for all departments. It is staff. So are personnel and public relations departments. They serve functionally in specific areas across organizational lines.

In something of the same manner, the Convention has set up agencies which interrelate in the same way for the good of all. Basically the committees, commissions, and institutions are staff in their relationships. The boards are line in their operations. Together they make a complete package.

Many of the institutions are housed in Nashville, Tennessee, but this does not mean that there is too much centralization in the organizational life of Southern Baptists. The fact that these are located in one city means geographical concentration but not organizational centralization. While they are located in the same city, each serves under a different controlling board, and each board is directly accountable to the Convention. Organizationally, except for the convenience of constant intercommunications between agencies in close proximity, they could just as well be spaced out in just as many cities as there are agencies. Centralization occurs when all are under one controlling body other than the Convention itself. Southern Baptists have studiously guarded against centralization of powers. Unless charters, the Convention constitution, and bylaws are all disregarded, movement toward organizational centralization in the denomination is only remotely possible, if not impossible.

Examine the four types of organizational structures used internally in the Southern Baptist Convention to get its vast work accomplished. These are:

Committees

A committee in the Convention functions in a way unique to itself. Other agencies operate quite differently. But a committee is set up with few or no specific powers to act on its own. If such authorities are granted, these must be spelled out clearly and be specifically defined. The basic way a committee works is to do what is usually referred to as "legwork" for the Convention. Mainly its assignments are to examine, evaluate, and recommend. Convention actions are required on each recommendation specifically before it becomes official. None of the committee decisions are final or authoritative. Committees are not decision-making bodies, but they are fundamental to the smooth operation of any deliberative body. Without the refining process provided by committees, the full body would not have enough facts in hand to make adequate judgments. These committees which serve the Convention on a continuing basis even when it is not in annual session do a very important and necessary work. They are of four types:

Executive Committee of the Southern Baptist Convention

We set the Committee apart here even though it is a standing committee. We do this because of its importance to the operation of the Convention and all its agencies. It is not only unique but indispensable. Its members are among some of the most capable, dedicated, and hardworking Baptists to be found in the entire denomination. It is desirable that they be capable of objectivity because of the overall nature of their work, even though the work to be done is basically analytical. It consists in the formulation of recommendations to the agencies or about the agencies and concerns itself with the general work of the Convention itself.

The Executive Committee analyzes, hears appeals, and makes recommendations in matters of budget and program and many other related matters. Still their major actions can be implemented only by approval of the Convention, making it necessary that the Executive Committee have more time on the annual program of a Southern Baptist Convention meeting than any several other agencies combined would require. It is authorized to handle unassigned matters which arise between Conventions, but it is the "Convention ad interim" only in unassigned areas. It can audit agencies directly, if some business area of that agency seems to be handled in a questionable manner. Usually, however, it receives and consolidates the audits and reports of all the agencies when they are duly prepared and filed with the Executive Committee to be placed in the Book of Reports which this committee prepares for the Convention.

In an ongoing way the Executive Committee distributes all funds, Cooperative Program and otherwise, as instructed. They issue news releases under the Baptist Press imprint in order to keep Baptists and others informed about movements in Baptist life. They assist in correlation and coordination of all programs assigned by the Convention to individual agencies to help them toward maximum achievements and efficiency as they serve in the Convention's life.

The Executive Committee, while it is not the supervisor of the various agencies, is still the Executive Committee of the

Southern Baptist Convention and deserves the maximum respect and support from all the agencies. If, however, it occasionally were to overstep its boundaries of assignment, the agency involved could be expected to refer it to the constitution and bylaws or request that the matter be debated on the Convention floor. Agency executive heads must operate by the minutes of the trustee meetings of the agencies they serve, not by the minutes of the Executive Committee, important as they might be. This keeps responsibilities and relationships in proper order according to Convention mandates. Only when the Convention itself acts are the agency trustees obligated to make readjustments.

As is true of all Convention committees, institutions, and boards, the trustee group, by whatever name it might be called, is elected by the Convention and made up of men and women, ministers and laypersons, from a widespread geographical area according to Baptist population in the state conventions from which they have been selected to serve. But all are elected by the Southern Baptist Convention, not the state Baptist conventions.

Standing Committees

Certain committees are called "Standing Committees" because they operate the year around, not only during Convention annual sessions but during all the months in between. They meet several times a year and do the delicate work assigned to them, reporting back to the Convention their evaluations and recommendations for action. They serve on rotating bases so that two-thirds of the members will be experienced in the techniques required of the committee at all times.

One of the standing committees is the *Denominational Calendar Committee,* which works closely with the Inter-Agency Council, as well as the SBC Executive Committee. It lists calendared activities so as to give balanced emphasis to all areas of work in an appropriate manner.

The other standing committee is the *Committee on Order of Business* which recommends the agenda for the annual session of the Southern Baptist Convention. This committee works hard before the Convention begins, in order that the recommended agenda might get wide publicity through all Baptist publications and be presented to the Convention for approval at its first session. Its most intense work is during the Convention meeting itself. The Committee on Order of Business is responsible for the timing of each agency or committee report, for extension of time when needed, and for the scheduling of times for debate when motions are introduced so that interested persons can be sure to attend at that time if they wish to participate or listen to the public debates.

Special Committees

There are two special committees. One is the *Committee on Boards*. This committee is recommended by the Committee on Committees which is appointed by the Convention president. This roundabout process is intended to keep any president at any time from wielding too much influence on the Convention. The Committee on Committees will have been named by the Convention president for the year before. That committee names the Committee on Boards which in turn will recommend board members, trustees, commissioners, and committee members who will guide the destinies of all Convention agencies between sessions. This is a most important committee, demanding the utmost care in selection. Under no conditions should it ever be a "stacked committee" for the purpose of producing a certain type of action!

Specific demands are made of the Committee on Boards concerning the type of persons they will place in nomination. An appropriate mix of ministers and laypersons is required. The committee is to carefully examine the personal qualifications and eligibility of each person whose name is submitted. Although not required to by the constitution, the committee is expected to give broad representation, providing for varying viewpoints on each of the boards and agencies in order to precipitate discussion in an ample manner as business matters are being handled. Without careful attention to this necessary mix of representation, institutions are more apt to err in judgment as their work progresses.

A *Committee on State Baptist Papers* is named to keep the fact of their importance in public focus continuously. The Southern Baptist Convention itself has no one Baptist publication which issues official positions of or for Southern Baptists. It is felt that a few dozen energetic, capable journalists, writing objectively about things as they see them, will be far more helpful than some authoritative publication which easily could come to assume more authority than intended. Although the state Baptist papers are owned and operated by state Baptist conventions, they are set up to serve the entire denomination and all the agencies in a very significant way. Their importance cannot be exaggerated.

Committees Relating to Other Baptists

Two Convention committees are different in nature from the ones already discussed. These are set up in the normal way, but they do not work exclusively within the Southern Baptist Convention organizational framework. Rather they represent our denomination in areas where all Baptist groups need to work together to accomplish that which no one Baptist group could do alone.

The *Committee on Public Affairs,* named by the Southern Baptist Convention, joins other comparable committee members elected by other Baptist groups to give special attention to the preservation of religious liberty in America as expressed in the first amendment of the Constitution. If and when laws are proposed or freedoms are threatened, this committee is obligated to speak out, alerting all Baptist groups of the need for awareness and remedy. The main office of the Baptist Joint Committee is in Washington, D.C., where a complete staff serves full time.

The *North American Baptist Fellowship* is the unit operating under the umbrella of the Baptist World Alliance to serve as a vehicle of communication with all other Baptist groups in the continental United States. The meetings are not only for the purpose of understanding, but they give opportunity for leadership in the various Baptist groups to know each other personally, as well as to study similarities and differences in programs, practices, methodology, and beliefs. These functions are important to all groups.

Commissions

There are seven commissions serving Southern Baptists, all of which specialize in their specifically assigned areas in most significant ways. These are different from committees, institutions, and boards. Yet their research, opinions, and assistance are often sought inside the Convention and out.

Commissions operate in a staff relationship in the Convention's organizational framework. They deal generally with functions more than actions. Their work is pinpointed in specifically stated duties, so they might be likened to "rifles" pointing all of their energies in one direction. They are most helpful in research and special emphases, in the molding of public opinion, and in doing specific assignments where specialization is necessary.

The *Education Commission* is set up to serve Baptist institutions of higher learning, although colleges are operated by state conventions rather than by the Southern Baptist Convention. There are many areas of need, however, that the states cannot provide for themselves. The Education Commission can tabulate information and share it among the colleges, assist them in information about possible personnel for teaching posts, and handle problems of continued accreditation and other such matters. Their work is thus highly significant and specialized.

The Southern Baptist *Commission on the American Baptist Theological Seminary* works with the National Baptist Convention, Inc., a Black Baptist body, in the operation of a school of higher learning located in Nashville, Tennessee, and jointly supervised. Historically, the American Baptist Theological Seminary has been a training post for Black Baptist pastors. Its influence in this area is still profound.

The area of the *Brotherhood Commission* assignment is missions, providing programs and activities for men and boys. It majors on missionary education and the locating and using of missionary resources and energies.

The *Christian Life Commission* is in a sense the "voice of conscience" of Southern Baptists stressing high moral and ethical applications and continuous practical implementation of the gospel. Their work is often controversial in nature because many of the assignments of the Christian Life Commission are in areas where public opinion has not yet crystallized and where emotional issues are still under heated discussion.

The Christian Life Commission is especially helpful in dealing with problems such as abortion, alcoholism, racism, dope addiction, and other matters of such nature. Even the introduction of organ transplants through surgery raises moral questions such as "When is the person dead?" or "At what stage can organs be removed from a human body while those organs are still alive, without it being considered murder legally or morally?" In these areas of public conscience, the Christian Life Commission functions with skill, giving guidance not only to the Convention but to the agencies which have to deal in some way with the subjects they have researched.

The *Historical Commission*'s area is to preserve history and to make Southern Baptists aware of their heritage and the necessity for recording it correctly for posterity. They work with all the historical societies which have gathered materials and data for generations. Their historical writings help us as a denomination as we seek to understand ourselves. They assist churches and other Baptist bodies in the best methods of recording and preserving history. They are especially helpful to graduate students or others preparing papers or dissertations in the area of Baptist history.

The *Radio and Television Commission,* like the other commissions, works in a pinpointed, clearly defined area demanding specialization. Its work is with the public media, helping Baptists get out the Good News, and rendering help to churches which broadcast and telecast their services on a regular basis. It is hoped that this service can enable them to present their programs with dignity and technical skill.

The *Stewardship Commission* also works in the specific area of giving, primarily with and through the state executive secretaries who have a major responsibility in promoting stewardship through their state conventions. The Stewardship Commission's work is very important. They do wonderful things in the area of publicity and stewardship emphasis. They give professional guidance in fund raising as needed by churches and institutions. They seek to create an awareness of the importance of Christian giving in Christian living.

Institutions

There are two types of Southern Baptist institutions, educational and financial. The *educational* institutions are the theological seminaries. They are highly scholastic and are geared to training ministers, missionaries, and other church workers. We have noted that colleges, academies, and Bible institutes are the responsibility of the several state conventions. Theological education is an assignment of the Southern Baptist Convention because the graduates are apt to serve in several parts of the nation or world. Therefore, they can be given a broader perspective in education in an institution operated by the national body. Originally the seminaries were limited to ordained ministers, and the entire curriculum was theological in nature. Greek and Hebrew were required. Indeed before a student could graduate and receive a graduate degree, he had to take every course taught by the school. As time passed, however, there was need for more optional courses at the seminary level of training, and many valuable courses are now available to the students. Later more trained ministers of education were needed to serve the larger churches, so courses were offered in that field, and music courses were added, also. Eventually these functions evolved into separate schools within the theological institutions so that most of the seminaries now have theological schools which specialize in training for pastors, religious education schools which train for general educational and training programs within a church, and schools of music which train leaders in the field of music in order that they can build and direct full-scale music programs for all ages where such is desired in a local church. In general usage, *religious education* refers to the educational work within a local church, and *Christian education* is the term generally applying to Baptist schools and colleges of higher learning.

The level of teaching in the seminaries is appropriate for college graduates. However, courses and even separate schools have been introduced to assist persons not quite so fortunate in their educational backgrounds, especially the ones who felt called to the ministry after they were mature in age and had families for which they were responsible.

The purpose is to help each seminary student to his or her highest potential in preparation and service. The nature of the degrees given graduates in the seminaries differs according to the number of years required in residence for courses to be taken. While the basic purpose of the seminaries is to train pastors and local church workers, they have such high academic records that the graduates can be admitted to universities throughout the world for advanced academic training beyond that provided by our own theological schools. This is necessary to those who plan to be teachers in colleges and theological schools located all over the world.

Listed according to the dates of their founding, there are six Southern Baptist theological schools:

1. The Southern Baptist Theological Seminary, located in Louisville, Kentucky, 1859.

2. Southwestern Baptist Theological Seminary, Fort Worth, Texas, 1908.

3. New Orleans Baptist Theological Seminary, New Orleans, Louisiana, 1917.

4. Golden Gate Baptist Theological Seminary, Mill Valley, California, 1944.

5. Southeastern Baptist Theological Seminary, Wake Forest, North Carolina, 1951.

6. Midwestern Baptist Theological Seminary, Kansas City, Missouri, 1957.

The way God has blessed the seminaries of Southern Baptists is indicated by the fact that nearly one-fifth of all theological students of all denominations of the nation are in the six seminaries owned and operated by Southern Baptists.

And it is well to note that these seminaries are widespread geographically, giving their students more opportunities to serve in student pastorates of the local area while getting seminary training. Continuing theological training is given those desiring it for academic credit and periodic refreshing in basic theological courses.

The six seminaries conduct a major portion of their off-campus training through the Seminary External Education Division. This channel for cooperative work is funded by the seminaries and small tuition fees from participants.

An entirely different type of Baptist institution is the *Southern Baptist Foundation*, a financial institution, set up to handle endowment funds, bequests, reserve funds, and many financial matters related to Southern Baptist Convention life. The Foundation serves in a very helpful manner, especially in its relationship to older couples and individuals with accumulated funds who have come to find the handling of their finances too much of a strain in their latter years. Many of these persons have few or no close relatives. They wish to leave their assets to some religious cause, but they need monthly financial incomes from those assets during their lifetimes. The Foundation will manage the funds according to agreement and issue income on a regular agreed basis to the individual or couple to meet their needs of old age and then dispose of the funds as directed after death has occurred. These funds may be designated for endowment of some institution or cause in which the donor has a special interest, or they can go into a general fund to be distributed somewhat like the Cooperative Program. The establishment of foundations is relatively new in Southern Baptist life, but they are rendering a unique service in meeting long-felt needs. The Southern Baptist Foundation seeks to do its work in harmony with Baptist foundations in the state conventions, some of which are older and larger than the Southern Baptist Convention Foundation set up to do its work on a national basis.

Boards

The boards of the Convention are the oldest, largest, and most complex of the denominational institutions. We have said the commissions were designed to operate like rifles, with specific impact at one point. By contrast, we can say the boards are more like shotguns in nature, big gauged, with scattered shots, doing work in many but related areas. The boards are fundamental to the welfare of a healthy denomination. In history they have been most efficient and effective. The two mission boards, the Foreign Mission Board and the Home Mission Board, are the two oldest agencies of Southern Baptists. They have been established as long as the Convention has been in existence. Both have and do serve well.

The Foreign Mission Board

The work of the *Foreign Mission Board*, housed in Richmond, Virginia, is easily defined by geography. It is the agency doing all types of mission work in many countries outside the United States where a Southern Baptist witness is needed and as funds are available. Outside the United States it is the exclusive agency representing Southern Baptists. It works with many governments. It operates schools, colleges, seminaries, hospitals. It helps establish churches and missions. It has preaching and teaching missionaries. In countries where preaching and teaching missionaries are not allowed, it sometimes succeeds in getting a Christian agricultural worker located. It sponsors all types of educational and publication work according to language needs around the world and conducts and sponsors radio and television programs wherever possible. In fact, it uses every available tool to get the gospel preached to the ends of the earth for churches affiliated with the Southern Baptist Convention.

The Foreign Mission Board selects missionaries, carefully supervises them, cares for them adequately after they are sent out and after they have retired. Fair salaries for services rendered are paid according to the value of money in the area to which missionaries are assigned. Southern Baptist missionaries are also equipped with excellent tools to do their work. It was more than just an incidental remark when an impoverished, poorly equipped, self-appointed missionary said on one occasion, "Southern Baptists are the Cadillacs of the mission fields." What he meant was that they are well prepared and adequately cared for when compared to representatives of other denominations who must work with such limited resources. It is fair that this be done, as the work and the workers are recognized for their importance.

Approximately one-half of all designated Cooperative Program gifts, as well as special missions offerings totaling multiplied millions, are assigned to the Foreign Mission Board for use each year. The mission advance of Southern Baptists is thrilling to behold. Still, one feels burdened when one contemplates what still remains undone. Like the early disciples of Christ, Southern Baptists continue to feel the weight of "the world" on their shoulders and hearts. This must remain a chief burden of Baptist people everywhere.

The Home Mission Board

The *Home Mission Board* has a work somewhat comparable to that of the Foreign Mission Board but limited in territory to the United States. Each state mission board does its own mission work in its own state. The Home Mission Board does its work in cooperation with them.

The work of the Home Mission Board is getting more complex all the time because of an ever-enlarging influx of many and vast ethnic groups who still speak their native tongues. So the language problem of the work in the United States is similar to but not quite as complex as that of the mission work abroad. The Home Mission Board was set up to be the "Domestic and Indian Board" in 1845, and as its name implied, majored on proclaiming the gospel to the Indian tribes. That work continues, but many other areas have been added, and the geography has expanded from coast-to-coast. Once the mission field was small in which Southern Baptist churches operated, primarily in the South, Southeast, and Southwest. Now the work is nationwide in scope. As society gets more complex and other needs arise, its work expands accordingly.

As a mission board, with the name coming from the Latin word *mitto* meaning "to send," its life has always been and remains centered in the mission thrust of Baptists within the nation. It serves as an agent of the churches to get the gospel preached and churches established in areas where the Baptist witness is small and the churches scarce and struggling. Its church loan funds help new churches secure needed buildings so that Bible teaching and adequate worship facilities can be provided. It operates rescue missions, works with mission departments in state Baptist conventions, and pioneers in the field of penetrating the inner cities where the population of people is so compacted.

So the work of the Home Mission Board is with the remote areas of the nation where Baptists are scarce, as well as in the concentrated areas where populations are intensely dense. Reaching and ministering to migrants who follow the harvests northward each year is one of the most romantic works done by the Home Mission Board. Its work is also supported financially by something like one-fourth of the Cooperative Program funds being sent through the Southern Baptist Convention. Added to that are sizable Home Mission offerings given annually during special weeks of prayer. The Home Mission Board, originally located in Marion, Alabama, has long since been moved to Atlanta, Georgia.

The Sunday School Board

The *Sunday School Board* of the Southern Baptist Convention is an entirely different type agency, majoring on religious education programs and publications designed to assist local churches in their Bible teaching, membership training, administration, and worship programs. In some ways the work of the Sunday School Board is similar to that of the Home Mission Board. They both operate over the entire United States, for example. In other ways, it is exactly opposite. People who do not understand the nature of each of the boards and the way they function may get the impression that they work constantly at cross purposes. Not so. They work in closest possible correlation and coordination, but their approaches are from different perspectives, indicated by the fact that the Home Mission Board is supported by Cooperative Program funds while the Sunday

School Board is not. The greatest difference, however, lies in the basic purpose and mode of operation of the two institutions. The Home Mission Board, as previously stated, is the agent of the churches to do mission work where those churches cannot go in order to do Baptist work directly where needed. In other words, it works in a direction away from the local church, making it a true mission board doing direct missions over the nation.

The Sunday School Board, by contrast, was established to serve those churches and their local Bible teaching, worship, and membership training needs. It is not a mission board and, therefore, does not receive mission gifts for its operation. It works with churches as they reach out to bring in people within reach of the local church. Therefore, the Sunday School Board promotes "outreach" programs, while the Home Mission Board promotes "mission" programs. Just as the Home Mission Board is a mission board working *from* the churches, the Sunday School Board might be looked upon as the *"local"* church board doing its work toward churches, assisting them in doing their own local work. With this philosophical and organizational difference, the thrusts of the two boards might seem quite different, and yet their work is done in harmony. In areas of overlap, they must stay in constant communication, each understanding the other completely. They seek to do this. The areas of overlap require detailed planning and constant meetings of the personnel involved.

The Sunday School Board's work is primarily in the field of religious education and promotion and the handling of service programs rendered to churches as needed and requested. It must work closely with all state Baptist conventions and district associations, as well as with all churches in the development of programs and materials. While it is owned and operated by the Southern Baptist Convention, it is set up to serve the entire Southern Baptist denomination in all areas to which its own assignment might be related.

Before there was a Sunday School Board churches got their Sunday School materials wherever they could. They were appealing for help. Editors of Baptist papers tried to get into the field, even though most of them were privately owned. Dr. J. M. Frost, founder of the Sunday School Board, saw intense difficulty, if not fragmentation, ahead because terminology and methodology are inherent in the production of Sunday School materials. With many publishers, there would be so many methodologies and such a diversity of terminology that a person moving from one state to another would be completely at a loss to use the new literature. Dr. Frost's desire was for all literature to be produced for use in all Southern Baptist churches regardless of location. Then when a person moved to another state he would have the same literature and doctrinal expressions, and the literature would not make him feel that he had entered another denomination. He could pick up where he left off, starting the next Sunday with the same literature and age group. This was the motivation behind the establishment of the Sunday School Board in 1891.

To accomplish his objective, Dr. Frost visited every participating Baptist state convention in Southern Baptist territory. He made each one a proposal that if it would participate in a program fostering the use of Sunday School literature produced by the Board among the churches of that state that the Board would share a part of the earnings from the sale of literature with the state conventions. The support was unanimous, and thus was born the idea of appropriations to state Baptist conventions. It still continues. This current year the amount appropriated for cooperative efforts of educational and promotional work with state conventions was $1,720,978.98. In addition, the Board is contributing this year $555,000 to Southern Baptist Convention support. This working agreement is another illustration that the Sunday School Board was set up to serve the entire denomination. It also points up the efficiency with which the Sunday School Board operates. No other major religious publishing house carries such a financial responsibility, and still the Sunday School Board literature is cheaper than comparable materials published by any other major denomination of the nation.

While the term *Sunday School* is still in the title of the institution, and at the beginning was appropriate, there are now at least two dozen other areas subsequently assigned to the institution such as Church Training, Church Music, National Student Ministries, Church Administration, and such, making the name antiquated. Then there are service areas like Church Architecture, Church Recreation, and Church Library Service. There are conference centers like Ridgecrest and Glorieta. There are publishing areas like Convention Press and Broadman Press, and distribution areas like the Baptist Book Stores, campus stores, and others. All areas of the work are supported financially by the sale of products. As discussed above, the Sunday School Board assists the state Baptist conventions in financing and furthering their departments and programs which are related to the Sunday School Board assignments. During all of Southern Baptist history, for example, all Sunday School Departments, Church Training Departments, Church Music Departments, and Student Departments of all of the state conventions have been funded in whole or part by the Sunday School Board.

While thousands of churches other than Southern Baptist use the literature produced by the Sunday School Board for Bible teaching programs, these materials are produced and intended for Southern Baptist use. Convention Press is the press name for books which are purely for denominational use and are distributed exclusively through Baptist Book Stores. These are books of the nature of *Building a Standard Sunday School,* which would be of interest to Baptists only. Broadman Press is different. It produces books of a general nature, and its products are distributed through hundreds of other book store outlets in addition to our own Baptist Book Stores. A book on prayer, for instance, should be of interest to people of any or all denominations. It would be produced under the Broadman Press imprint for general distribution from its broader base.

The Sunday School Board is headquartered in Nashville, Tennessee, but operates the nation over through its book stores and conference center services.

The Annuity Board

Any compassionate denomination will be concerned about its faithful pastors and church workers who have served the Lord well for years and have come to old age. Their latter years ought to be as secure and comfortable as possible, because employment and constant income will slow then or will be no longer available. It was this concern that brought into existence in Dallas, Texas, the Relief and Annuity Board, which is owned and operated by the Southern Baptist Convention. In time the word "Relief" was dropped from the title, and the institution became known simply as The Annuity Board of the Southern Baptist Convention. It concerns itself with the development and management of pension funds, on bases in which the individual, the church he or she serves, and the denomination make regular payments to build up accounts which are to be returned in the form of pension payments after the workers' retirement. In later years, health programs have been introduced and are available to pastors and full-time vocational church workers in the denomination.

The Annuity Board's problems become acute in eras of inflation when living costs accelerate because payments into the funds were made when costs of living were much lower. Yet it has difficulties in depression times also when payment into the fund becomes more difficult. Fortunately, some of the best Baptist minds available in the nation have been pooled to develop plans which could provide maximum funding for any eventuality. Perhaps the most nagging concern the Board has is that so many pastors in the churches express little concern for retirement plans of any kind until retirement becomes imminent. Then, after it is too late to store up adequate resources, the people and churches involved tend to become desperate. The Annuity Board historically has been noted for its compassion as well as its businesslike manner of operation, but what it can do must have been worked out long before the retirement years approach if retirement funds are to be adequate. The work of the Annuity Board in its truest sense is Baptist compassion at work in a practical way for its own religious workers.

An Example of Cooperation Between Agencies

Even though evangelism has been assigned to the Home Mission Board as a program, we have reserved until now any discussion of how that assignment relates to the other agencies so that the Home Mission Board's Evangelism Department can be considered the "captain of the team" in the field of evangelism with all of the resources of the entire Convention holding important positions on the team and working toward the common goal of soul-winning. Even in evangelism, the techniques used by the Home Mission Board are different from those used by the Sunday School Board.

Having served personally on a special study committee appointed by Dr. Louie D. Newton, then president of the Southern Baptist Convention, to deal with the appropriate location of the Convention's evangelism responsibility, I saw the present situation developing and the relationships and philosophies being worked out which are still appropriate. The state evangelism secretaries who met with this special committee in Dallas in the 1940s had the unanimous feeling that the major Southern Baptist Convention evangelism responsibility should be fixed as an assignment of the Sunday School Board. They felt the major work of evangelism at that time was being done through the Sunday School movement. Too, the Home Mission Board's evangelistic thrust had been primarily through specially named evangelists sent out to hold revival meetings in areas where evangelistic needs were the greatest.

At the end of this special committee meeting in Dallas, I was asked by the committee to be their representative to confer with Dr. T. L. Holcomb, then executive secretary of the Baptist Sunday School Board, to see if he would be interested in supporting their recommendation that the evangelism responsibility be placed with the Sunday School Board. In carrying out that request, I was told by Dr. Holcomb that it was his personal feeling that while the Sunday School Board had tremendous responsibilities in the area of evangelism, and would continue to the best of its ability to fulfill them, the major thrust of evangelism should be from the Home Mission Board, instead. His comment was that if the major thrust were fixed with the Sunday School Board primarily, when it is more educational in nature, that over the years people might gradually get the impression that a person could be educated into the Kingdom of God. He felt that the major thrust should be from a strong mission base rather than an educational base. He recommended that we propose that the responsibility be assigned to the Home Mission Board. That was done, and the relationship remains.

While the Sunday Schools of the land must be evangelistic in spirit and practice on a continuous basis, and while the Sunday School Board is deeply involved in evangelism in every way possible, still the "captain of the team" in evangelism is the Home Mission Board, coordinating all efforts nationwide. It must not, however, be overlooked that every agency of the Southern Baptist Convention has its evangelism assignment fixed by the Southern Baptist Convention. An agency's very reason for being is expressed at the outset of its program description with a statement like, "The Baptist Sunday School Board exists for the purpose of bringing men to God through Jesus Christ, by . . .," and then the specific program statements are appropriately inserted. In other words, every major agency of the Southern Baptist Convention has as its major reason for being a responsibility in evangelism. Nothing could be more fundamental than that this major assignment be properly understood and implemented. Nothing could be more tragic or costly than for this to be overlooked or for the Home Mission Board to assume that evangelism is its responsibility exclusively, to the exclusion of the other agencies.

The evangelism secretary at the Home Mission Board cannot do his job alone, and with the wrong viewpoint could actually jeopardize the evangelistic work of the other agencies, which have proper assignments in the same field, specifically made by Convention action. The evangelism secretary at the Home Mission Board is to work with and through all areas, agencies, units, and resources of the denomination to give the most dynamic thrust possible in all evangelistic endeavors. Indeed, there are areas which must belong to all agencies, who are to give their continuous and full support. The areas which must have promotion and the support of every existing Southern Baptist Convention agency are evangelism, stewardship, and missionary education. To divide up these responsibilities tends to paralyze the movements.

The paragraphs above illustrate the necessity for closest possible communication and cooperation among agencies in the promotion of kindred endeavors. They illustrate how agencies must and do work together. Such cooperation is necessary in the entire denomination affecting all other agencies.

It is easy to define certain assignments with clarity, but there are inevitable overlapping areas which cannot be delineated. Even money and organizational skills cannot solve some problems, so the best possible solutions must be sought on a continuing basis. To illustrate, even the army with all of its money and power is faced with an unsolvable problem. Everyone knows that the foot soldiers operate on the ground and that the air forces operate in the sky. As long as the soldiers are on the ground and the airplanes are in the air, there is no problem of overlap. But the hard fact is that the airplanes that fly above must come to the land where the foot soldier is. At that point the army and the air force must talk and work out plans jointly to prevent catastrophes. In this same way, agencies must stay in constant communication in areas where delineation of duties cannot be clearly and lastingly defined, in order that each might render maximum service without conflict. Correlation refers to the planning process. Coordination refers to harmonious relationships as those plans are being carried out. Unless communications are constant, there is a tendency for both agencies involved to do one of two things, both of which are bad. Either both will back away to stay out of each other's way, or both will move in and clash head-on. Each method is ineffective.

For a number of years, the Inter-Agency Council has helped with the work of correlation and cooperation between the agencies. While the Inter-Agency Council, made up of an equal number of representatives from each Convention agency, has official standing, it has very limited privileges. It was set up in the late 1950s to help correlate the programs of the agencies, but it can bring no recommendation directly to the Convention floor. Its recommendations must go to the Program Committee of the Convention's Executive Committee and through that committee to the Convention itself for authoritative actions.

Conclusion

It is obvious that we have given only a brief kaleidoscopic glance at each agency of the Southern Baptist Convention. To detail the work of even the smallest agency would require the entire chapter. To give all details of the larger ones would demand the entire book. The purpose here has been to present at a glance the main duties and relationships without benefit of details.

You will notice again by the chart that the committees, commissions, and institutions major on functions and serve the Convention from a staff relationship much like accounting and personnel departments operate in a corporation. The boards serve in a line relationship majoring on actions. This viewpoint must be kept in mind before the basic agency relationship can be understood or kept in balance.

8

An Annual Convention: Participation and Cooperation

A Baptist can view Baptist polity in action by attending an annual meeting of the Southern Baptist Convention. Since there are thirty-four state Baptist conventions and more than twelve hundred Baptist associations, it is impossible to detail exactly how they all do things by our mentally visiting any of them. Methods of operation are too different among them for that. We can, however, mentally sit in on an annual session of the Southern Baptist Convention to see how it works as it serves the churches admirably in bringing to pass certain things in which the churches have special interests.

It is hard for some of us who have attended Southern Baptist Convention annual sessions for forty to fifty years to realize that the majority of Baptists have never seen a Southern Baptist Convention session in progress. One of the amazements in the Convention year-after-year comes when the president asks those who are in attendance for the very first time to lift their hands. Fully one-fourth of those attending any particular year will be there for the very first time.

The vast majority of those attending every annual meeting of the Southern Baptist Convention will be pastors or other members of local church staffs. Maybe this is to be expected, but sometimes it can create problems. The Convention is made up of messengers sent from the churches, but no church in the Convention is made up of 70 percent or more of ministers of the gospel, as the Convention is. So, the Convention is never exactly typical of the nature and needs of any local church. While the denomination is always strongly lay-oriented, the Southern Baptist Convention meetings are without exception strongly minister-oriented. This sometimes presents a problem, especially when some messengers from churches want the Convention to express itself in ways the denomination might not approve. But somehow God has steered us through this difficulty time after time.

While the annual session of a typical Southern Baptist Convention will last only three days, certain Convention groups, and especially the Southern Baptist Convention Executive Committee, will be at work all year to assure smooth Convention operations.

For the sake of interpreting the annual Southern Baptist Convention in the briefest possible form and for the sake of those who have never attended, we want to mentally run through an annual Convention meeting in order that the nature and happenings can be understood and appreciated.

Far in Advance of the Meeting

The most advanced planning is done by the Southern Baptist Convention's Executive Committee as it explores cities for possible Convention meeting places as well as dates. Since there are now only about a dozen or so cities in America large enough to house, sleep, and feed the multitude of messengers, and provide adequate meeting places for the many related gatherings on acceptable dates, details must be scheduled several years in advance. The hall must be large enough to seat tens of thousands of messengers and provide exhibit space for all the agencies and the Baptist Book Stores. Hotels must guarantee enough rooms to meet the needs of the group. Restaurants must be many in number and nearby in area. Most of all, the local Baptist people must want the meeting in their city and be willing to provide enough local workers to man the many local committees necessary to carry out meetings of such tremendous proportions.

After two or three cities are explored as possibilities, all facts are discussed by the SBC Executive Committee which will decide on the one place that seems most feasible. With all the facts in hand, they will recommend the place of meeting deemed best some five or seven years ahead. Usually the

Convention will go along with the recommendation, but occasionally they will change it. An example was the Norfolk, Virginia, meeting in 1976. The messengers had rejected the recommendation of the Executive Committee and expressed the preference to endure the hardships of meeting in an undersized auditorium, with hotels scattered from Norfolk to the Atlantic coastline, as well as other major limitations, in order that the messengers might meet in this historic area of our nation's beginning during the Bicentennial Celebration.

The necessary ad hoc committees, though named to serve many local functions until the end of the oncoming Convention, are set into motion under a local arrangements committee which gives overall guidance and detailed planning in the city in which the Convention is to be held. Executive Committee personnel are so experienced in these matters that they can recommend to the local leaders the type and number of committees needed and the number of persons necessary to fulfill the needs of a convention of such tremendous size.

The Committee on Order of Business is set up on a rotating basis by the Convention. It begins early to develop the type of program that it will recommend for the next year so it can be announced at the appropriate time. This committee plans and gives wide publicity to the proposed program through all denominational papers after it has taken shape, but well in advance of Convention time. The Convention usually meets for three days and nights, with afternoon programs planned for Tuesday and Thursday only. Wednesday afternoon is the time reserved for seminary luncheons, local sightseeing visits, receptions for missionaries, recognition dinners, and meetings of this type. These, while not official parts of the Convention, usually occur during Convention week and are important in the denomination's life.

Ordinarily business activities are handled during the morning and afternoon sessions, along with the Convention sermon and one or two inspirational addresses. The evening programs may have brief agency reports, but they tend more toward the informational and inspirational type of presentations with pageants and dramas stressing mission needs and denominational actions. Customarily the closing session will feature a world-renowned speaker, preceded by a colorful program emphasizing the coming year's theme or thrust.

A number of related meetings, set up just before the Convention, have massive attendance and influence Southern Baptist life greatly, although they are not actual parts of the Convention process. They come then because it is a good time to meet and because the expense of another journey to another nationwide assembly would be too great. Especially should we note that the Woman's Missionary Union holds its annual session on the days immediately preceding the Southern Baptist Convention, a historic custom which has existed over many decades. Other meetings provide time for fellowship and learning experiences for religious education workers, musicians, chaplains, evangelists, and a host of other similar groups in specialized meetings with programs prepared specifically for them. Colleges, and many state conventions and agencies, join the Southern Baptist Convention agencies in presenting massive and attractive displays to feature all aspects of Baptist life and work. These are all scheduled and planned well in advance, also, but are separate from the Committee on Order of Business, which is addressing itself to the planning of specific Convention programs and activities.

The many related meetings which immediately precede the annual Convention meeting are generally helpful. They provide inspiration as well as information in many specific areas. These meetings are not officially related to the Convention and generally have strengthened the Convention's work. Only rarely has the Convention been hindered by actions and emphases issuing from these pre-Convention meetings. In fact, I can remember only a couple of times in all of my years when the Convention's objective handling of problems was impeded by actions of these prior meetings. Both had to do with the Baptist Pastors' Conference. On one occasion it appeared that certain activists sought to use the organization to promote a slate of proposed Convention officers. In doing so they used the organization unwisely in attempting to influence Convention decisions.

On another occasion, a seminary textbook published by Broadman Press became such an issue in a Pastors' Conference that not one single speaker or leader in prayer failed to call the name of the book's author in some way, making objective dealing with the matter practically impossible when the issue finally came to the Convention floor. And this was done even though there were no remaining copies of the book in the warehouse, and instructions had been given that no additional copies were to be produced except on approval of the full body of trustees (board members) of the Sunday School Board in official session.

Anytime a pre-Convention meeting seeks to influence subsequent Convention action in a negative way, it is operating apart from its reason for being. Its officers must judiciously guard against such actions.

Since each agency is owned and operated by the Convention, each one has a time set aside to report its stewardship of responsibility to the full body covering the year just ended. Since the Convention's purpose is to handle business through those responsible agencies, time must be given for adequate reporting by them, or the Convention's basic purpose is compromised. These agencies deserve to be heard, and if necessary, redirected. Unless this process is followed, the agency trustees and the administrators have heavy responsibilities thrown upon them which were never intended and which they do not want or deserve.

The annual sessions of the Convention for the first hundred years or more were scheduled during the last half of May. So much time was demanded for travel from distant parts of the Convention to the meeting city, that it was rare indeed for family members, especially children, to accompany parents to the annual Southern Baptist Convention sessions. In addition, commencement time for local schools came about the same time of the Convention's meeting, making it impossible for high school students to accompany parents each year.

As time and travel facilities progressed, and as churches expressed their desire to send their pastors and their families to the Southern Baptist Convention meetings as a gesture of love and appreciation, appeals were made for the meeting time of the Convention to be shifted into June to make this possible. In this way, young people even in high school could attend after school had dismissed. This was done. Attendance increased drastically because there was more of a tendency for pastors to come with family groups. Both good and bad have resulted from this practice. It is wonderful for a pastor to be able to have these intimate times of fellowship with his family, sometimes almost prohibited at home by the intense schedules of local pastorates. On the other hand, the practice at times has produced overcrowded convention halls, hotels, and restaurants with so many nonvoting members attending each year that problems of housing messengers have resulted. Even more difficult, parents who bring small children cannot usually attend all Convention sessions. The children must have breaks from the convention halls periodically, which means that some messengers occasionally miss critical sessions which they would like to have attended and in which they were needed. While nurseries and day-care centers ease the problem to a degree, they have not solved it.

There is a purpose in rotating from city to city from year to year. Records show, and experienced messengers have observed, that the largest number of persons attending any Convention session have come from nearby churches and states. This is intended and desired, but the fact must not be overlooked that it also tends to make any one Convention session somewhat sectional or territorial in nature, which can vitally influence the decision-making process. Since different areas of the nation may view things differently, even among Southern Baptists, plans must be made to prevent sectionalism from manifesting itself in important Convention actions and decisions.

The way of dealing with the problem of sectionalism is for the Convention not only to alter its place of meetings from time-to-time but also to require that constitutional changes cannot be made until they have been ratified in two successive annual Conventions. In part, this is to force deliberate changes to be made with objectivity. A constitutional change made after being approved at two successive conventions in different parts of the nation will not have been unduly influenced by regional factors. The ensuing policy will take on nationwide characteristics. Meeting in different cities is not for convenience only, but for strategy reasons as well. At the same time it gives more people opportunity to attend at least one Convention during their lives, when the Convention's annual meeting is in their part of the nation.

Prior confirmed lodging reservations are almost mandatory before messengers leave for the Convention meeting. Getting rooms after arrival is next to a miracle. This is all handled through a housing committee, with hotels, locations, and costs being well publicized in advance through Baptist state papers and *The Baptist Program*, published by the Executive Committee of the Southern Baptist Convention, and sent to pastors and Convention leaders. The earlier these reservations can be confirmed after the announcement has been made that the Committee on Housing is ready to receive applications, the better it is for the messengers. To be on the safe side, it is best to pay for one night's lodging in advance in the event travel plans are interrupted and late arrival becomes unavoidable. In this way, the reservation will be held.

Another item to be handled well in advance is the official election of messengers by the churches from which these messengers are being sent and in which they currently hold membership. There is no legitimate way to claim "honorary membership" or to register from a church where one's membership is not placed at the time. Ten is the maximum number of messengers from any church, regardless of its size. Regardless of their smallness or age, all cooperating and contributing churches can send at least one messenger. The rest of the churches can determine their number of eligible messengers by studying the Convention's bylaws and doing a bit of calculating. This number is determined by size of membership and gifts and varies from time-to-time as the Convention sees fit to alter its plan for registration. What must not be overlooked is that all messengers must be duly elected in business session in their local churches, and that registration cards must be presented at the registration desk after having been signed by the pastor and/or moderator or being confirmed by official letter or telegram. Without one of these, no messenger is officially accepted as a messenger with voting and discussion privileges. Registration cards can be secured from a district Baptist associational office or a state convention building.

Another of the earlier actions must be taken by the president of the Convention who has the responsibility of setting up certain ad hoc committees which will assist in registration, credentials, resolutions, ushering, and so forth.

One of the important items is for the president, in consultation with the registration secretary, to select the tellers who will conduct the voting procedure when officers are being elected or when vital issues are being determined by ballot. All of these ad hoc committees must be set up before the Convention and be ready to launch into full-scale movement at the strategic time.

During the Convention Sessions

Once the time has arrived, things must move with clockwork precision while some twenty thousand messengers will be in official attendance. Some thirty thousand people will come to the meetings, because the visitors average about one-third of the attendance. They are not voting members but attend along with the messengers. They may be husband, wife, or friend. Nothing related to planning an annual session of the Convention can be left to the last minute, or the problems flare and flame furiously beyond control in an instant under the pressure of such massive attendances.

Registration is usually begun the day before the Convention for the benefit of the ones arriving early, but it continues throughout the Convention for the benefit of late arrivals. Sometimes pre-registration is made possible by mail. The registration card not only lists the Convention's rigid requirements which will qualify a messenger for registration, it also lists the place of lodging where the registrant will be staying during the Convention so that he can be notified in the event of an emergency. The registration secretary keeps this exacting responsibility of registration coordinated and the cards filed by states. As the Convention wishes, it may check the cards by computer to determine that the churches have sent the right number of messengers and that no one has exceeded the allowable quota. There are no provisions for substitute messengers from any church to act when elected messengers are away.

Upon registration each messenger is given a badge for personal identification, identifying the state from which he has come. A Book of Reports is also given, consolidating all official reports of the agencies to the Convention. A batch of unused ballots is also included. Ballots have been tediously prepared to assure that all voting will be according to required procedure. They are prenumbered and prepunched so only one card can be used for each balloting. In fact, the computer will reject cards if they are not the right ones each time a vote is taken. This forces one vote by the one person who is a messenger and allows no other. Having someone else vote in the place of a messenger is forbidden, so the use of more than one ballot each time is eliminated. In this way, the Convention can be assured that the processes are in order and that the votes cast are truly official. Messengers vote by punching out the appropriate square as instructed. Results are available immediately, providing an instantaneous report of returns on the voting.

The Convention proper begins on Tuesday morning of a Convention week at 9:00 AM, but it is usually preceded by thirty minutes of special music by a school or church choir while the messengers are arriving and are being seated. At exactly 9:00 AM the president is required to call the Convention into order, announcing the number of years the Convention has been in meeting annually in past history and which one this year is in the line of historic sequence. He then introduces the music director who leads a song which will be followed by a Scripture reading and prayer by well-chosen participants. Usually the ones who read the Scriptures and lead in prayer are from some particular or select group. They may be missionaries, laymen, laywomen, or retirees. This procedure sets the tone of worship which is so vital to a Convention's spirit and effectiveness. At this point the registration secretary will be introduced. He will make a motion which not only announces the number of registered messengers at the moment of beginning but officially constitutes them into an organized, deliberating body for official business. The statement made by the registration secretary will be something like, "Already twelve thousand persons have been duly registered, and I make the motion that these messengers constitute the Convention and that duly accredited messengers from the churches in cooperation with the Convention who arrive late be recognized as members of the Convention when they have enrolled on the basis of membership set forth by Article III of the Constitution." With a vote approving this motion, the Convention is officially underway. Unless the Convention is meeting in some city far removed from the center of its constituency, the number of messengers will ordinarily reach fifteen to twenty-two thousand before adjournment time has arrived.

At the outset, the Committee on Order of Business presents its recommended agenda on which it has worked for months to assure balanced reporting with a fair allotted time being granted to each speaker and agency. The theme of the Convention has been kept in mind so that there will be a central idea throughout the week.

Bylaw 28(3) requires each agency to set aside one-third of its allotted time to hear and answer questions from the floor. Since each messenger has a printed Book of Reports in hand which he should have read before the Convention starts, if possible, the agency may offer one-third of its reporting time at the beginning or at the end of its reporting time. With the report read in advance, either way is satisfactory. Usually discussion or question time comes at the beginning so that the balance of the allotted time can be used to maximum advantage in the systematic presentation of the agency's work for the year just ended.

Each agency report is expected to give a clear interpretation of the institution's achievements according to program assignments given it by the Convention. These programs reported on by the agencies are actually "possessions" of the churches and do not belong to any agency or to the Convention itself. However, the programs are committed to the Convention by the churches for strengthening by united actions. The Convention in turn fixes responsibilities for these programs with agencies under the guidance of carefully elected trustees and with a systematic plan laid out for annual reporting and readjustment as desirable. In due time reports are made back to the churches so that they can know in detail what the Convention and its agencies are doing in the light of their assignments as they relate to the expressed desires of the churches.

Specific times in the agenda will allow for miscellaneous business. This is when any qualified messenger can present a resolution or a motion if he wishes, if he feels deeply about any subject or area of the Convention's life and work.

One of the hardest working committees of any Convention will be the Committee on Resolutions. It has been named well in advance by the president, representing the Convention's broad geographical spread and the diversified church memberships, to encourage open discussion within the committee. The members of this committee seldom get to attend many sessions of the Convention except the one where their own committee report is made, because so much time is required in their own meetings and open hearings that there is no free time left. If more than one resolution is offered on any given subject, the Committee on Resolutions consolidates them in an effective way. A resolutions committee might consider one resolution to be effectively stated and appropriately presented and recommend it word-for-word as it was given. Others will be revised or consolidated. Still others will be bypassed, because they do not seem to be appropriate, or because the Convention has expressed itself on that same subject at an earlier time. The committee does not have to report back on every resolution submitted. Its report and recommendations are according to its own best judgment. Resolutions committees frequently reword resolutions to fit what they assume to be the deepest needs of the Convention.

The resolution is first presented to the body not by full reading but by a simple statement giving the nature of the resolution to the full body of messengers. The full copy is then placed in the hands of the Committee on Resolutions. If it is brought back to the floor of the Convention, it is at that time presented in entirety, as each word is carefully weighed before and by the body. If someone objects to the way the resolution is altered by the Committee, he can debate the wisdom of that change on the floor of the Convention as the time allows and if the president recognizes him.

So many resolutions are being presented from year-to-year during these current chaotic times that methods are now being sought to make this part of Convention agenda more orderly and efficient. Perhaps it can be done by developing a screening process requiring a certain number of signatures on a resolution before it can be admitted for consideration by the Committee on Resolutions. But Baptists are very hesitant to limit the free expression of any messenger at any time. Changes in this area are not easily made. As a result, much time is consumed in dealing with resolutions, as its many subjects are handled in detail one-by-one.

At the very first miscellaneous business time of a Convention, (1) resolutions and (2) motions may be offered by any messenger. These two are different in nature, and the Convention president must determine on short notice which each is and declare publicly its proper routing.

A *resolution* takes a position and is automatically referred to the Committee on Resolutions to be dealt with at a later time as just discussed.

A *motion* calls for an action. When a motion is made, the president declares it to be that, and the Committee on Order of Business is required to set aside a specifically announced time in the agenda for the discussion and consideration of it. In this way, anyone wanting to enter into the discussion of a particular motion knows in advance when it is to be handled. He can then be present and be prepared for participation if he wishes.

Because of the rapid-fire speed of resolutions, motions, motions to amend, substitute motions, and many other parliamentary procedures, the naming of a parliamentarian is permitted. He is usually considered essential to assist the president in making split-second analyses of a situation and a proper parliamentary decision.

The president must keep matters moving with dispatch and yet stay completely in control. A parliamentarian is of indispensable value in that regard. While there is a parliamentarian to help analyze and discuss possible alternatives for the president, the decisions made are always by the president and are to be considered his responsibility. Frequently, he does need a parliamentarian's interpretations along with some suggested viable options he might exercise to avoid further confusion on the part of the body. The parliamentarian historically has been named by the president, although he may be elected by the body if the body chooses.

When open discussions are in progress, the president will alternate speakers according to whether the person is for or against the motion before the body. Microphones are strategically located over the halls in easy reach by messengers regardless of where they might be seated. A red light on top of the microphone signifies that a person at that microphone is wishing to speak. Those persons are recognized in the order in which lights flash to catch the attention of the Convention president, who is the moderator of the meeting. The president, of course, is the one who exercises judgment as to whether all sides of an issue have been heard adequately. He is free to express that judgment to the body although the messengers may vote to extend time and continue a discussion if and as they wish.

The Convention historically has been very slow to cut off debate unless every angle of an issue has been adequately discussed. Usually that point can be determined when the speakers begin to repeat what previous speakers have said.

Persons unfamiliar with Southern Baptist Conventions are usually amazed that debates can be so systematically handled with so many potential speakers in attendance. But it needs to be remembered that every messenger does not need to speak on every subject. Instead, speakers need to be heard only until every side of an issue has been presented so that voters can cast their ballots intelligently. This means the same amount of debate time is required for twenty thousand potential voters as for a few hundred messengers. So the size of the body really does not change matters materially. It is the nature of the motion or issue at hand which determines the amount of time required for consideration, not the number of messengers who have registered. Very seldom does one feel that he has been "cut off" from debate. But when such has been done, it is due to the fact that the allotted time for debate has expired, and the president or Committee on Order of Business feels that all of the pertinent facts are before the body. As a result one of them will decline to recommend an extension of time. Even then if debate is cut off it is done by a vote of the full body. It is amazing that things can be so open and free with so many participants and so many subjects under consideration.

There was a time when physically seeing and hearing Convention speakers was difficult. They were so far away. Both of these hardships have been overcome in remarkable ways by use of modern technology. Even though the meeting halls are large and oftentimes have flat floors, modern-day audio systems are most sensitive to sound and can be controlled easily by professionals so that every person can hear well regardless of where he might be seated. The same is true of the giant screens, usually three in number, which project the images of the speakers and participants to the farthest corners of the hall with the greatest of ease. Once the messengers have become accustomed to these modern methods and facilities, the systems become an accepted part of the process. Everyone seems to become unaware of their existence as the Convention proceeds systematically.

One of the most exciting parts of each Convention is the election time for new officers, especially on those years when the current president is finishing his tenure and cannot succeed himself. Attendance is usually at its highest when elections are in progress, when controversial matters are up for discussion, and when missionary reports are being given.

The persons nominated for the presidency usually come from different states, representing various segments of Baptist life, or are connected with various movements and trends within the Convention itself. Laymen are nominated often but regrettably are seldom elected. It is more difficult for laymen to become well known on a Convention-wide basis, a necessary factor before a Convention is apt to elect one to be its chief officer, the president. The person elected president is a person in whom the messengers feel they can put their trust at that particular time to meet the issues of that particular date. And these issues and circumstances shift from time to time, which means that the characteristics of the people elected to this office will also vary. He (or she) must be capable of objectivity and fairness in presiding skills. It is preferable that the president be a good speaker, but this is not a requirement. Two years constitute the maximum consecutive term of any president.

The first vice-president is usually a person of similar age and skills as the president himself. He is a person chosen with the view that he can readily step into the president's chair if some emergency should arise making the continuation of the current president's tenure impossible.

The second vice-president may be the same type of person, well known and deliberately chosen with the view that perhaps the president and vice-president could both suffer debilitating misfortunes. More often, however, the second vice-president is someone elected because of a special recognition the Convention wants to give or a special service already rendered. To illustrate, the second vice-president is frequently chosen because of having just served as chairman of the local arrangements committee while the Convention was meeting in that city. While women, Blacks, Hispanics, and others have been elected to the vice-presidency, as of now all of the presidents have been white males, and usually pastors. The vice-presidents from time to time preside over the meetings when the president needs a rest period or when the president is called aside for meetings with the press or for purposes of taking official photographs.

There is no time limit to regulate the terms of service of the remaining officers who are: recording secretary, registration secretary, and treasurer. Usually these three offices are filled by the same person year after year because of special technical skills required to do their particular work. The recording secretary is responsible for keeping accurate minutes of the meeting and preparing copy for the printing of the *Convention Annual* for the preservation of official history of Convention sessions. The treasurer has always been the same person as the executive secretary-treasurer of the Southern Baptist Convention's Executive Committee, although it is required that he be elected as treasurer annually.

Throughout the duration of the Convention there are ushers, nursery workers, persons directing parking, persons handling displays, choirs, soloists, and many other persons and items moving or being moved according to plan. They move in such an organized and skillful way that the average person in attendance is hardly aware of the many things involved in the smooth operation of an annual session of the Southern Baptist Convention. This is evidence of good organization and planning. Royal Ambassadors who have achieved high ranks will usually serve as pages for the Convention officers. They sit on the platform. Baptist editors and agency executives sit at desks immediately in front of the platform on the main floor.

Daily bulletins are produced throughout the Convention time, detailing all matters related to the Convention. The bulletin calls attention to things yet to come and interprets things that have already transpired. When motions are made or resolutions offered for consideration, they are printed in full in the bulletin so that they can be studied word-by-word in order to produce the clearest communication possible. All announcements are made through this particular daily bulletin.

News media will be represented by dozens of reporters who have set aside the week to attend the Southern Baptist Convention sessions and to report in detail on its happenings through their papers or on radio and television. Baptist Press representatives are especially busy interpreting to the press and public media what the meanings of special actions are in order that they can properly report them to others.

One of the puzzling things to Convention newcomers is to observe one Convention action that they have seldom seen back home. For example, officers of the Convention must be elected by ballot. This is required. But what do you do when only one person has been nominated? Do you ballot? Such procedure consumes time and is unnecessary. As a result, the body will entertain a motion to instruct the recording secretary to "cast a ballot" in behalf of the one person nominated. When such a vote has been taken by the body, the recording secretary steps to the podium with words such as, "It is my pleasure to cast my ballot for John Doe for the first vice-president." It is done by ballot, therefore, as required by the bylaws, and much time has been saved in the process. It is an interesting procedure seldom seen elsewhere.

Most Southern Baptists will never be privileged to sit in on an annual meeting of the Southern Baptist Convention as a messenger or visitor. If all could, each would be pleased at the fairness shown each messenger, as with impartiality each one is given opportunity to express viewpoints freely. At the same time, extremisms are usually discouraged by the very process of democracy. If an extremist persists in speaking prejudiced and unjustified views, a deliberative body will soon recognize his off-center positions. This person will tend to lose his influence immediately on that body. They will hear him, but they will cease to respect his views, if he has moved very far from the center of the constituency in assembly.

After the Convention Is Over

Because of the nature of the Southern Baptist Convention and its relationship to the churches, no Convention vote is binding on any local Baptist church anywhere. Each church is just as free to act after a Convention session as it was before the Convention met to express itself. But it is good for each church to know how the majority stands on a given issue or question in order that it might make proper decisions on its own in the light of those expressed judgments.

Agencies take into account pertinent Convention actions relative to them and their work. All Convention actions related to the agency's work will be automatically referred to the trustees for consideration. The chief executive officer does not take direct action based on Southern Baptist Convention actions. He must act on trustee minutes alone. So Convention actions are referred to the trustees who discuss ways in which they think Convention actions relate to them and state their judgments in the agency minutes. At that point, the administrator steps in to seek to implement the actions trustees have taken. Sometimes it is a tedious process requiring considerable time. But never have I known a Convention agency to disregard or defy a Convention action which was referred to it. For this reason, it is seldom expected that the Convention will take an action "instructing" an agency to move in a certain way. Usually they suggest that trustees "give consideration to" a certain matter. In other words, they cast the general direction, leaving details of implementation to the trustees.

One of the most helpful procedures as far as agencies are concerned is that any motion made from the floor of a Convention concerning the inside operations of an agency will be automatically referred to the trustees of that agency. The trustees must not only deal with this matter of reference intelligently but are required to report back in detail their disposition of the matter at the following Convention. The wisdom of this procedure can be understood when it is remembered that occasionally motions have been made from the floor of the Convention which have dealt with matters already under study or consideration by the trustees of an institution. For the Convention, not having all details in hand, to try to deal with such a situation would more likely intensify the problem and slow down an ultimate satisfactory solution.

Messengers of the Southern Baptist Convention are "two-way" messengers. They go as voices of interest and concern from the churches *to* a Southern Baptist Convention. Once that Convention is over, they then become voices of communication *for* the Convention to the membership of the churches which have sent them. Time should always be set aside within a week after each annual session of the Southern Baptist Convention for messengers who have attended to give brief overall oral reports of their experiences and impressions of the Convention. It is better still if the church also sends a state Baptist paper into every church home, because in that way detailed reporting can be given and impressions studied which have been prepared and presented by skilled Baptist editors who are now giving their professional but objective evaluations of happenings.

Conventions are expensive to hold. They are more expensive not to hold. At stake is the autonomy of the local church, the soul freedom of all persons, and the democratic processes by which these precious heritages can be preserved. So they are "musts" in our Baptist process.

We could say that without annual conventions the work of our denomination would be slowed down immeasurably and the worldwide witness would be handicapped. Business meetings, local and national, are necessary to an ongoing process for Baptists.

9

Understanding
the Trustee System

Law requires that each chartered institution be operated under trustees. In this way the government can know the official name by which the institution is called, who owns and operates it, and who is to be held responsible for its actions. The institution must have authorization to buy, own, and sell property, as well as to acquire debts and be responsible for paying them in due manner.

Fortunately, these requirements are in harmony with the Southern Baptist system of owning and operating its institutions as they assist churches in the fulfillment of their Christian duties as New Testament-like bodies. There is no practical way our Convention could operate its institutions except through trustees, unless it were willing to stay in constant session. Even then it might be impossible. Fortunately, the complexities of administering a large institution can be fixed with trustees in whom the Convention has complete confidence. In this way, constant reporting and evaluation can be carried out by the full body to make sure the original purposes of the institution are being fulfilled and that it is not veering from that original purpose consciously or unconsciously.

Of course, the state Baptist conventions, which own and operate institutions like colleges, hospitals, and children's homes, will follow their own systems of institutional operation and management; but in each case trustees are required, and the system works. In this chapter we must focus on the Southern Baptist Convention and its method of operating its boards, agencies, and institutions in a responsible manner. It boils down to a directed system of delegation operating under close and constant scrutiny but with enough elbow room allowed for the institutions to exercise initiative and creativity within the bounds of specific limitations. It works out to be almost an exact science, providing efficiency and effectiveness while at the same time the institution moves and serves in a specific way doing an exacting work of utmost importance.

Trustees are in a very real sense the persons selected by the Convention to whom they feel they can entrust their institutions for managing and operating the way the Convention desires and directs. Under law, the institution or agency may be considered to be owned by the trustees. But under Southern Baptist polity, it is owned and operated by the body which elects those trustees and sets the institution's course of action and system of accountability.

Institutions are necessary to the strong operation of any effective denomination. They are like fortresses to an army, guaranteeing stability and a sense of permanence. But they are costly and time consuming. Institutions are dynamic, fast-moving, and strong. They do a tremendous good when fulfilling their assigned responsibilities but can do irreparable harm if they get out of hand and veer from the purpose for which they were brought into being. Thus trustees must be carefully selected, constantly alert, and fully loyal to the owning body as well as to the institution they are serving as trustees. Trustees need to be representatives carefully chosen for their diversified viewpoints and unquestioned loyalty. Differences in individual viewpoints within the trustees will force discussions necessary for the filtering out of error and guaranteeing the best possible solutions by which the institution can reach its optimum effectiveness.

How trustees can be chosen and function to help institutions reach that maximum strength of purpose seems like an unsolvable jigsaw puzzle to some people, until it is analyzed with clarity. Actually, it is a very simple process, effective and consistent, and proven by the Southern Baptist Convention to be a most effective way of helping the individual churches fulfill their massive responsibilities through institutions. That service to the churches must always be kept in mind by every institution owned and operated by the Convention, since that is basic to the purpose of the Convention itself. An institution's work in Baptist life is the work of the local churches assigned to that institution. It is not free to do as it chooses.

Because institutions are so important and influential in Southern Baptist Convention life, extra care must be taken in the process by which trustees who direct them are elected. Diligent effort is put forth to keep "Convention politics" at a minimum when they are being chosen. The seemingly roundabout way trustees are elected, therefore, is not accidental but purposeful, and it serves a necessary function.

Here is the way the process of trustee election works. The outgoing president (or the president with only one remaining year of tenure) names a Committee on Committees. In turn that Committee on Committees nominates the Committee on Boards, made up of one minister and one layperson from each state convention territory. The Committee on Boards then nominates trustees for the boards, agencies, and institutions of the Convention. The names of the nominees are published in advance of their election so the messengers can gain more information about them if desired.

All trustee groups for all agencies must be balanced between ministers and laypersons, with at least one-third from each classification. It is hoped that they will vary in age and viewpoints so as to encourage discussion in board meetings. Both men and women need to be represented.

All trustees are elected by the Convention in official session and are accountable to the Convention for all actions and decisions. Their tenure is designated at the outset, and they can serve only two full terms. They may or may not be reelected for a second term, as the Convention wishes.

Trustees will be chosen from state convention territories, but they are expected to have Southern Baptist Convention-wide perspective. They are not necessarily representing the states where they reside but may report prevailing viewpoints at meetings.

Trustees must remember that all Southern Baptist Convention agencies exist to serve the churches in the fulfillment of their functions, which is the basic purpose of the denomination itself. Therefore, the purpose of the agency they direct must be kept in mind so it will be Christian in nature, ever aware of its spiritual purposes. The process of election is designed to give diversity in trustee selection, which is necessary in a denomination like ours.

In seeking a simple way of describing the trustee system and how it works, let us start by showing the gradation by which the system is set into operation. Certain specific things must be done at approved levels before other accomplishments can be considered. The Southern Baptist Convention's control of its institutions' charters and its election of their trustees assure its control of its own institutions and agencies and their work. It can operate with confidence and still give the institutions the degree of flexibility they need to be efficient operations. If a convention dares to make all of its decisions from the floor of the convention, it renders the trustees powerless in their decision-making process. Too, such a procedure would mean that when errors do occur, the convention must accept responsibility for them and not the trustees who have been bypassed in their direct responsibilities. No one wants that. Institutions simply cannot be run from the floor of a convention.

In our effort to understand how the trustee principle works, let us take a parallel from the field of athletics— basketball, a game we all see frequently and understand well. Let us see how it has developed and operates. In that way, we will have a visible picture giving us a parallel to the way institutions which are less visible are begun and function.

First, before anybody plays basketball, some responsible group must meet and develop the overall system by which the game is to be played. They actually determine the science of the game and write its rules. They determine the number of players each team shall have, the size of each court, the height and size of the baskets, the size and weight of the balls, and other such important matters. Their work is general in some ways but very specific in others. No one at any other level can reverse or change their decisions. All is done from an objective point of view to make the game fascinating to the fans as well as the players. No school, coach, or player can write these rules or make these determinations. They are made for him before he ever becomes a player or before the school plans to sponsor a team.

Second, a school then can decide whether it wants to play the sport or not. This decision has to come after the earlier decisions have been fully determined. The school that wants to participate in basketball must agree to play by the rules, build a gymnasium, appropriate money to finance the teams, choose the school colors, determine the relationship between academic achievements and athletics, decide whether scholarships shall or shall not be given, and employ a coach who will be in general charge of the implementation of the school program of basketball.

Third, the coach begins at that point to select the players, buy the athletic equipment, choose the players on the basis of merit, select the system by which the team will develop its plays, name the ones who will start each game, and make substitutes during game time as the situation warrants.

Fourth, the players do their playing totally within the framework of all the previous steps. They come on the scene at this point to elect their captain, accept responsibility for the building of team spirit, determine the zeal with which they are to play the game, and determine to follow the coach's guidance to the best of their abilities.

Not to be overlooked is the fact that in spite of all the actions taken thus far, the players still must be left certain freedoms of action in playing the game, or nearly every game will be lost. While players must understand and respect the rules and seek to play by them, they cannot be expected to look to the coach each time and ask permission to shoot a basket. Privileges within limitations are built into the system in order to produce creativity and the fulfillment of responsibility. Constantly to "breathe down the necks of the players" and give them no opportunity for self-expression would be to defeat them before the game had begun. No player will feel free to exercise his own initiative and carry out his own talent in fullest measure unless he can play the game the way in which he himself feels comfortable.

Up until now, we have gone somewhat into detail to point

out that there are four gradations of control in the building of
basketball. At each level certain things are done by different
groups, until finally we come to the specifics of the play on
the court. The referee blows the whistle when the rules are
broken; this is required, or the game gets out of hand. But
the referee must not be a player. He must do his work,
always, from an objective, impartial point of view.

The operation of institutions by the Southern Baptist
Convention must follow essentially the same course. It
means that the Convention is to control its own affairs,
including the setting up of its own institutions; but it also
means that creativity and initiative should not be stifled
within those institutions lest they become impotent and
immobile. Institutions cannot fulfill their purposes unless
they are left to do certain things certain ways within the
framework of the limitations predetermined by the Convention, but free nevertheless so the workers can feel comfortable in their work and rewarded for their efforts.

Never can the players of a basketball game feel that they
are free to play the game in any way they choose. The same
type privileges and limitations are automatically imposed
upon every institution Southern Baptists own, as well as
every individual employed by each institution.

To be healthy an institution must have both objectivity and
subjectivity. The subjectivity is inherent in the viewpoints
and attitudes of the workers, if they are to succeed. But
because of that subjectivity, they have limitations also because that same subjectivity tends to give the workers a
sense akin to possessiveness. But remember, that possessiveness disqualifies them for policymaking. It becomes like a
doctor whose child needs surgery. He may be a skilled
surgeon, but another surgeon must be called in to operate on
a surgeon's child. Subjectivity is good, but it has limitations.
Workers are so individually involved that they cannot be
objective in all the decisions they make internally. For that
reason, the Convention and the trustees are to provide the
objectivity. In this way trustees become like referees of a
basketball game. They can call the shots with impartiality
exactly as they see them. This process separates policymak-

ing or "the writing of the rules," from administration, "the playing of the game." Nothing will destroy an institution's effectiveness more quickly than for trustees to seek to engage in administration, or for the administration to seek to be the policymakers.

Institutions are set up by the Southern Baptist Convention similarly to the way basketball was first begun by the specialists writing the rules and later carried out by the schools electing to participate in the sport. The Convention itself determines or approves the charter of each and every institution, seeing that the approved charter is filed with the appropriate branch of government. It will be well to note that charters are usually very brief statements and are so broadly written that they speak more or less in general terms except where the law demands specifics. It is interesting to observe that the charter of the Southern Baptist Convention, approved in 1845, and filed according to the laws of Georgia, totaled only sixteen lines. The Convention also elects the trustees. This is a step that is never to be delegated to anyone else.

As in basketball, the second step is for the trustees to determine the details related to how the institution is to be run in order to fulfill the purpose for which it was given life. This is specifically detailed in the constitution and bylaws written by the trustees but in harmony with the charter which the Convention has already approved.

The administrator, or president if that is what the administrator is called, is elected to operate within the framework of a charter, constitution, and bylaws. He is to administer the affairs, but all is to be done in a specified way already spelled out. All of the administrative decisions must be within the framework of the previous actions at different levels. The chief administrative officer will come in at that point to recommend a budget, suggest how employees are to be selected or terminated, proceed to employ workers as planned, determine job descriptions, job evaluations, and salaries, supervise workers in their daily duties, and be responsible for producing that which the Southern Baptist Convention had in mind when the institution was first given

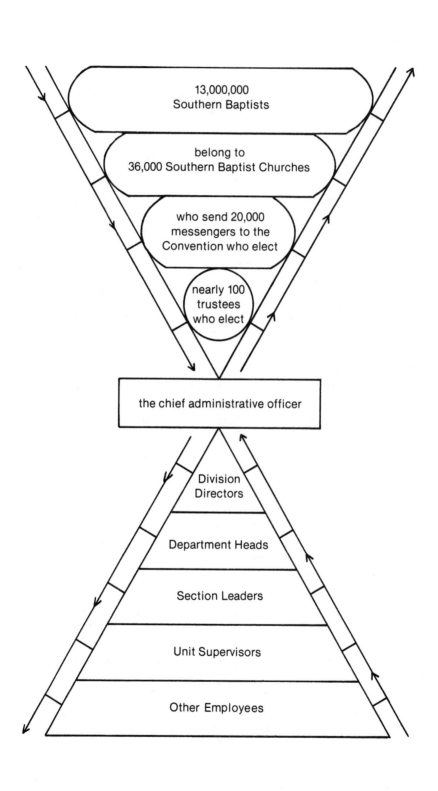

The chief administrator (president, executive secretary, executive director, or some other title) is elected by trustees who have been elected by messengers to the Southern Baptist Convention. They in turn were sent by the churches representing all Baptists. The administrator acts as the fulcrum of the operation to maintain balance, a sense of purpose, and optimum effectiveness of the institution in its stated purpose. He will have a staff of division directors who guide the work of the department heads. They in turn direct the work of section leaders who direct the activities of the unit supervisors. All workers are directly accountable to someone with the chief administrator coordinating the entire process, guiding the institution toward the goals set for it by the Convention. Job descriptions tell what each worker is to do. A procedures manual explains how the work is to be done and how each job relates to other jobs. Job evaluation tells how each position is rated for fixing salary schedules. Communication flows from the top to the chief administrator and back up to the last Baptist with a question. Inside directives flow from the administrator to all employees, and reports flow back to describe progress being made on the assignments. Input into the up and down flow is possible at all levels as shown by the short, slanted lines on the chart.

existence. In this way the Convention remains in control of its own affairs not only through the charter but through a regular reporting system to the body of messengers who can interrogate either the chief executive officer or the trustees on any part of the carrying out of the duties of the institution. It is a portrayal of stewardship in its best form as everyone seeks to fulfill the high purposes of the Convention. And the Convention exists to serve the churches.

With this background discussion and an athletic illustration, which we hope clarifies the nature of the charter, constitution, and bylaws, as well as the relationships of the chief executive officer to the employees, let us try to understand further the nature of the trustee system. Let us look at the chart given to point out how the trustee system functions by visualizing a giant X. This chart will show that there are some thirteen million Southern Baptists throughout the nation represented by the largest circle within the upper V. These thirteen million Southern Baptists belong to some thirty-six thousand individual local churches represented by the smaller circle immediately under them. These thirty-six thousand and more churches are eligible to send some twenty thousand duly elected messengers to an annual meeting of the Southern Baptist Convention, as represented by an even smaller circle underneath. The small body of trustees represented by the smallest circle has been elected by the Convention for specific responsibility and accountability.

Please notice the sequence of movements from the massive membership of individual Southern Baptist churches to the group of directed trustees who are held accountable for the institution's functioning and fulfillment of responsibility. To undertake to run the institutions by any of the larger bodies above would not only be bunglesome but impossible. Instead responsibility focuses gradually to the trustees who in turn elect a chief executive officer at the fulcrum of the X who will seek to carry out the wishes of the Baptist bodies above. The focus is thus fixed.

A chief executive officer may be called president, executive secretary, executive director, or some other title. He is the chief executive administrator directly accountable to the trustees who in turn have been chosen by the Convention which was made up of messengers sent from the churches. Through this sequence of communications and expressed wishes, the process can produce the type of institutions Southern Baptists wish most to have. If Baptist institutions are not unique, and if they do not fulfill the purposes of the churches, it is questionable whether their existence can be justified.

In the chart you will notice that there is a line of communication showing movement downward whereby communications are constantly fed to the institution from each level. On the other side of the X is the line with arrows pointed upward to show that there is returning communication through public relations programs, minutes, and other methods of reporting whereby the general constituency can be constantly informed to make sure that the wishes of the Baptist people are being carried out in an optimum way. The short, slanted lines symbolize the possibility of communication and input at every level in the pattern of relationships.

It is very significant to see the chief administrative officer as functioning from the cross point of the X. This shows how responsibilities are fixed in focus with him and how communications constantly go back and forth, to and from, the institution. All policy is determined above his office, and all administration is carried on at or below his office. He fits in at the fulcrum, at the crucial point of the crossing. He is the intermediary between the bodies above and the employees below, as well as the manager of all movements within.

The chief administrative officer has some degree of liberties, like a player on the basketball court, but all of his actions must be within clearly defined limitations previously prescribed. If he refuses to abide by these predetermined "rules of play," he must be declared disqualified to serve and be replaced. As harsh as this sounds, it is the only way Southern Baptists can stay in charge of their own institutions. Sometimes trustees may be reluctant to carry out the will of the Convention, and the same principle must apply there. The difference is that trustees can be replaced only by a slow-moving process. This is necessary in order to keep the Convention from operating precipitously and doing damage to itself.

One of the reasons why instantaneous corrections or changes cannot be made by an institution is that the processes can be complex. Because of the levels of authority, there are times when adjustments to bring about correction have to be made at every level. For example, if a change is desired, and the problem has been brought about by the way the charter is worded, time is necessary for correction. If that happens to be the case, the charter must be revised by the Convention itself before any other corrections or changes can be brought about either in the constitution or bylaws. This means that only when the constitution and bylaws have been rewritten can the trustees change their course of action. Until the trustees have revised their minutes, the chief administrative officer has no alternative except to operate the way the trustee minutes have been written. To change at all these many levels requires a period of months, or perhaps years. It still means, however, that the Convention is in charge of its own affairs, and changes can be and are brought about as the Convention wishes, given due time to do so.

It might be noted, also, that workers for institutions need to have some degree of tolerance or freedom in their operations, just like the basketball players, if they are to serve well. Institutions must learn by experience just as individuals do, and that experience calls for learning by trial and error—both of which are a part of the learning process. If an institution errs, there are some who may want to deal harshly with it instantaneously. This may or it may not be the correct action. If a chief administrative officer is replaced by some harsh judgment on the part of the controlling body above, causing a new person to be named, the new person may have to make the same errors again before he learns how to function there with maximum effectiveness. Such would also be the case with trustees. There is no such thing as a perfect institution, because institutions, like churches, are made up of people. People are imperfect, and it is impossible to have a perfect institution made up of imperfect component parts. If an institution becomes too afraid of error, it, like players in a game, will begin to get "butterfingers." In such a situation, players will mishandle the ball at nearly every point of crisis because they are too tense and afraid of failure. An athlete who is not willing to run the risk of mishandling the ball will never score in the game. Risk is a natural part of any operation, and this principle demands patience and a degree of tolerance while the workers seek to reach the highest possible level of their potential. Trial and error must provide for some degree of error in the learning process.

The chief administrative officer needs to respect another principle of a trustee system. He must act on decisions of *all* the trustees and not of any small segment within them. Technically speaking, a trustee is not a trustee until all of the trustees are in official session. Having discussed the matters at hand, and having written minutes recording their best judgments, the trustees adjourn. The administrative officer at that point can take the minutes and operate effectively by them. If, on the other hand, the chief administrative officer calls in one or two trustees and dares to operate off of their individual judgments and recommendations, his actions must be considered administrative actions for which the administrator is personally responsible. Trustees are responsible when their written decisions are carried out by an administrator. An administrator is responsible if he exercises judgment on his own. The only way for trustee action to be properly interpreted and followed is by the minutes that have been duly formulated, giving specific directions concerning the way the institution is to move next.

No institution of the Convention can have more authority than the Convention itself has. No Southern Baptist Convention can exceed the authorities granted by the messengers from the churches.

Trustees may be selected in the light of their particular abilities and aptitudes for service in specific places. Each institution of Baptists is different, and it takes a different type of person to render the particular services needed by that institution. Educational institutions need one type of trustees, and missionary institutions need another. Those that are supported by Cooperative Program gifts need one type of trustees, and institutions that have to supply their own funds with what they earn demand trustees who are more familiar with basic business principles. While all trustees are to be Christlike in nature and are to be members of Baptist churches, the individuals chosen must have specialized abilities that will make them sympathetic and supportive of the institution with which they are related and for which they are responsible. Hospitals do not need the same type of persons that a foreign mission board would need. Certain commissions would not demand the same type person to be a trustee that the Executive Committee would need as a member.

In order to have balanced trustees, the requirement of the Southern Baptist Convention is that the trustees of each institution be made up of both ministers and laypersons. The first group includes the ordained ministers and others serving full time on church staffs. All others are considered laypersons. The Committee on Boards ought to have a mixture of youth and age, men and women, new trustees along with experienced ones, progressive-minded persons along with cautious ones. Their decisions jointly reached, after deliberate discussion in trustee meetings, will then be more apt to stand the test of time and stress.

Trustees are usually elected for a stated period and then are automatically rotated off in order that new persons and new ideas might be interjected into the institution's life. It should be noted that trustees are rotated in a staggered fashion, not all at one time. This serves several good purposes. One is that it makes the institution more creative and alert, because the door is opened for a group of younger upcoming trustees gaining positions of influence in Baptist life, who will be elected to fill the vacancies. Without a rotating system, trustees tend to stagnate, feeling that all good ideas have been presented and implemented already. Such would be an unfortunate attitude on the part of any institution. Every institution must move forward constantly, adjusting to the times and finding better ways to render the services expected of it. Attitudes change within the churches, people are constantly seeking better ways to do things, and new ideas and approaches as well as new technological inventions are being made available. Every institution needs to keep alert and move forward as new doors open and as circumstances permit. But no institution should be allowed to stray from its original purpose or assignment.

The rotating system of trustees gives more people an opportunity to see the inside workings of an institution from a trustee's point of view. This provides more people on the field to interpret the institution and its missions to the people and churches in the vicinity of their residence. Too, a retired trustee is in a position to adequately and authoritatively answer questions in the area in which he has served well.

When problems do present themselves, or when tensions inside the Convention spill over into the institutions creating special problems, the trustees and the chief administrative officers must work cooperatively to understand the nature of the problems and to deal with them in a practical way that will allay fears and build confidence. Once the course of action has been determined, they should all move forward in unity and vigor to interpret the position of the institution and to ride through the turbulent times together. Those times come occasionally when there are no easy answers and when institutions must "nail down the hatches and ride out the storm" because the avoiding of turbulent waters for them at that point is impossible. Such experiences are never pleasant. They are often costly, but sometimes this must be done to rescue an institution in the time of blinding storms when Convention opinions are almost evenly divided and there are no clear-cut directives giving guidance to those who have responsibility. No institution which has existed over a long span of years has been able to escape these unfortunate and unavoidable problems in the ever-changing scene of Baptist life. Trustees are the ballast, and the chief executive officer is the pilot of the institution through troubled waters when turbulent times do arrive—and they will.

Generally speaking, the trustees of a Southern Baptist

institution meet twice each year, and more often if and when situations demand. Each, however, will have an executive committee of its own, which has limited authority to handle "nuts and bolts" responsibilities for day-to-day authorizations and guidance. The Convention agencies which operate on an interstate basis are subject to federal laws, even though they are religious institutions. Special legal authorizations are needed by the administration before certain other steps can be taken to meet those legal requirements. Trustees must approve these actions. Steps should be taken, if possible, before crisis situations arise. It is usually considered that actions taken in a crisis produce over-actions or reactions which can create problems of yet another sort. Solutions of all problems should be made intelligently and deliberately, never under coercive crisis pressures. In more than fifty years of service in the Southern Baptist Convention, I have never seen a trustee group who did not want to carry out the will of the Convention to the best of its ability as it understood the intent and purpose of the body. At times I have seen quandary as they tried to determine the nature and meaning of Convention actions, but never have I seen any manifestation of a spirit of defiance.

Under our system all dedicated Baptists will want the will of our Baptist people done. If they can only understand the nature of the directions being given, they will carry them out as best they can.

Before closing our discussions on the trustee system, we need to look again at the chart at the part of the operation below the chief executive officer. The institution, unlike the Convention, is a corporation. It must operate under a system of management to produce accomplishments for the churches, to fulfill the purposes for which the institution is brought into being. For that reason, an institution is not a democracy. Matters are not to be taken under consideration by employees to see whether they will carry out orders or not. In a corporate structure, like a Southern Baptist institution, the worker must either carry out the directives or seek employment elsewhere. It is just that simple. All democratic processes are taking place in the chart above the executive officer, none below him. Above him the question is "Wilt thou"? Below him the directive is, "Thou shalt." That is the difference between a democratic process and the operation of a corporate structure. For this reason some people are temperamentally unqualified to serve Southern Baptist institutions because they want to work as if the institution were a democracy. Such is impossible for Baptist agencies if the mission of the institution or agency is to be fulfilled.

The institution likely will be set up with divisions, departments, sections, units, and individual workers, but all are under supervisors with specific job assignments and procedures by which the work of each person is directed. Each worker is evaluated on the basis of efficiency and quality of work. Salaries are based on the worth and influence of a position and the way the responsibilities are carried out as well as the spirit shown by the worker in the doing of the job.

Notice, also, that the lines of communication go up and down on the administrative side as well as the policy side. Communications can flow to the chief executive officer at any time from any source, but where corrections are called for these must be handled organizationally, perhaps with trustee assistance. There are internal communications to be carried on constantly among all the workers in order that the work force can stay coordinated and efficient. Communications must be given by the chief executive officer which are clearly understood by every employee. Every employee's work is reported upward toward the chief executive officer. Through this institutional guidance system, the purposes of the institution can be fulfilled.

The health of a Southern Baptist institution has a direct effect upon the health of the Convention itself, and vice versa. When institutions are fulfilling their functions to the fullest, growth and a sense of accomplishment are felt throughout the entire body. This means that institutions deserve the prayerful support of Baptist people everywhere. Their effectiveness is necessary to a strong Christian witness around the world and to the Convention's rendering the services expected by the churches.

10

Financing
a Worldwide Movement

Baptist polity affects the way we give to Christian causes. The basic purpose of the Southern Baptist denomination is to aid and assist the churches in the doing of their work. In no place is this more evident than in the financing of the vast missionary-benevolent and charitable activities of the local churches carried on through the denomination in an ongoing and tremendously effective way. Such a movement would be too costly for any church to undertake alone, regardless of size or resources. Joint efforts and cooperative endeavors are necessary if the local churches are to do the work Christ laid out before them. But how are they to work together?

Three Key Words

A study of the charter of the Southern Baptist Convention reveals that the three key words setting forth the work of the Convention in 1845 are (1) *elicit*, (2) *combine*, and (3) *direct*. The wording as spelled out in the charter expressed that the Convention was "created for the purpose of eliciting, combining and directing the energies of the Baptist denomination." It is most important to observe that the basis on which the Convention was brought into being was not Christian doctrine, but Christian action. As necessary as doctrine is, it was not the original basis of our cooperation as a denomination. Not only was mission and ministry action the original motivation, it still remains the major emphasis.

We cannot know all that our forefathers envisioned when the Southern Baptist Convention was organized. A financial basis of representation was carried over from the society system. However, the key element in the society system— one society for each kind of ministry—was rejected in favor of putting all cooperative work under one convention. Although many society features were retained by Southern Baptists for a number of years, a new kind of organization had been born. The three key words just mentioned were important in the charter of the Triennial Convention and the charter of the new Convention. Looking back from our contemporary vantage point, we see how these words describe what came to be for Southern Baptists. When these three words are analyzed from this perspective, we discover, at least in embryonic form, the philosophy and methodology for cooperative action among Southern Baptists.

The first word is *eliciting*. The word does not refer to the assessment of a certain amount of money according to the size of a congregation. The ideal methodology for fund raising for Baptist churches through the Southern Baptist denomination was anticipated even in the original charter of the Convention. It implies that facts are to be presented, passionate appeals are to be made, proper motivation is to be sought, and then Southern Baptist people hopefully will give for the worthy causes spelled out as Christian duties for local churches. It is true that this statement issues from Bible teaching, but it is action-oriented. It calls for cooperative endeavors to be undertaken voluntarily in order to magnify Christian efforts and witness around the world. It stresses appropriate motivation among the people but does not imply manipulating people or churches simply for the purpose of getting money. Church members are to be led to want to give in order that mighty things may be accomplished which will be pleasing to God. Promotion can be done with insistence and persistence of effort, but all giving should be on a voluntary basis. This is a very important factor in denominational support.

The second key word is *combining*, meaning that funds given by the churches—working jointly to undertake the things they could never do alone—are put together to finance the causes determined. This concept produced the unified budget idea among Southern Baptists, a pooling of funds in order that adequate resources might be available to support worthy causes. This word was suggesting movement away from the trend of the times, which was for funds to go for designated purposes. Under the society system, nearly all funds were designated. Consequently, the causes with a deep emotional appeal, like children's homes, found fund raising relatively easy; but institutions with less emotional appeal, like theological seminaries, found the going exceedingly hard under that type of denominational administration. However, when all funds are combined into one, as through the Cooperative Program, they can be equitably distributed according to need, and all causes should receive adequate support in the process. Southern Baptists retained many society features after 1845, but movement in a new structural direction had been initiated.

The third key word is *directing*, meaning that the funds would be expended according to the wishes of the body in a way that would produce maximum results with the contributions received. Looking back, we see that these three words laid the groundwork for current Southern Baptist Convention cooperative funding. What we now have is quite different from the financing method of the old society system used by churches for many years. That plan, while it secured funds for operation, created many other problems, not the least of which was competition among the societies. Under the Southern Baptist Convention system the moneys would be pooled, and that common fund would support all worthy causes and would maintain support on a sustained level. The Convention system of denominational administration is different and refreshingly effective. As will be seen in the next section, the development of the Cooperative Program in 1925 brought this newness into its sharpest focus.

There seems to be only one basic change from this original concept as expressed in the charter of 1845. That is in the sequence of the words. The three words still apply, but the *distributing* is now detailed and authorized in advance, even before the *eliciting* and *combining* are undertaken. It is not a change in concept but in the sequence in which these three things take place. Today the giver can know in advance and in detail how the money which he is contributing is to be spent, and when one gives his money, it is directed to go in that way and no other. Southern Baptists are exceedingly cautious to make sure that money given for one cause will not be diverted into another channel to be used for a different purpose. Operating funds go for operations, as approved. Capital improvement funds go for building expansion and enlargement. Reserve funds go into reserves. A full accounting is publicly announced, and no one can change the authorizations given by the Convention for the expenditure of funds, except the Convention itself. Any Baptist can know in full in advance how each dollar he contributes is to be spent. Actually this shift in sequence of the three words is an improvement over the original concept, and the determination is made in advance as to how the funds will be used when received.

Occasionally some Baptists question the *directing* of the expenditure of funds by the general body. They continue to feel, perhaps sincerely, that each individual ought to, by designation, determine the distribution of gifts personally. They insist that this be undertaken. At first glance, one can see how complex bookkeeping would be under that sort of system. Bookkeeping is complex at best, even now, but with each individual designating every gift for dozens of causes, bookkeeping would become practically impossible. Essentially the same results are probably achieved by a group of people pooling all their funds and then voting on the distribution as if each individual designated all of his gifts personally. Interests differ, causing people who support one cause avidly to be less interested in another. So it stands to reason that combining and distributing the available funds probably produces similar if not identical final results as individual designation. And the process of "pooling" is much simpler, much cheaper, and fulfills the same purpose as individual designation.

The door is always open for any individual to designate his gifts if he wishes. When he does, these funds will be channeled into the various interests in which he has expressed his special concern. The bulk of Southern Baptist giving is undesignated and must stay that way if the Southern Baptist spirit of cooperation is maintained. However, any individual Baptist is still free to designate his gifts if he prefers to do so.

Development of the Cooperative Program

In 1925 the Cooperative Program was developed on the three key words as set forth in 1845 when the Southern Baptist Convention was first taking shape. It had taken eighty years for this original purpose to find its full method of operation. Even then there had been many intermediary steps taken by the churches experimenting with various concepts of giving, seeking to determine which was the best way.

In spite of the thrust toward voluntary support and united giving under Convention guidance as first envisioned, the Baptist people were still not trained adequately in tithing and systematic giving. Churches frequently were quarter time, with meetings only one Sunday in the month. They were periodic in their functioning, frequently operating only during the warmer months of the year when transportation was easiest. So developing biblical patterns of giving was slow among Southern Baptist leadership. This meant that the development of the people would be slow. To make matters worse, the Civil War flared and left the South, the area of predominant Southern Baptist Convention population, an impoverished area, where many churches ceased to exist. Even the surviving ones operated under great difficulty during the Reconstruction period when bankruptcy was practically universal. Solicitation of funds for foreign and home missions seemed imperative and was resorted to by the Convention leadership. The same was true of The Southern Baptist Theological Seminary when it came into existence in 1859. Field representatives literally lived on the field, seeking funds for support of the Convention agencies during that time. While solicitation was not the system envisioned by the Convention's founding fathers, it seemed to be the only method available at the time for the survival of the institutions, and so it was undertaken. For a painfully long time direct solicitation was the main source of raising funds for financing Southern Baptist causes. Gradually, solicitors were added by several state conventions, as was true in an increasing number of institutions which were begun and expanded.

When the denomination was young and small, the solicitation method seemed to work fairly satisfactorily. While never producing all of the funds desired, they did raise enough money for the institutions to survive and serve in a fairly efficient manner. As the Convention territory expanded and as Baptist institutions increased in number, the method of solicitation began to become a burden to the churches. So many solicitors were on the field that churches had visiting fund raisers several times each year, or oftener. In fact, solicitors came so often and appeals were made so frequently that pastors and congregations sometimes felt they were being manipulated, and they came to have a feeling of resentment against the denomination for the procedure being used. There were too many times in the year when the pastor could not occupy his own pulpit for which he was responsible. Solicitors expected opportunities to appear before the people to make their direct appeals. There had to be a better way. Too many people were competing for the same Baptist dollar, and churches felt they were being torn asunder. They were interested in all of the worthy causes but felt there had to be a method superior to the one being used. It is appropriate to note that the first insistence for a better system of financing denominational causes came from the churches themselves out of their own feeling of frustration and pressure.

Some churches undertook creative ways of meeting the problem and contributing to all causes with undesignated gifts. The church in which I grew up in Tylertown, Mississippi, voted in 1918, seven years before the Cooperative Program was set up by the Southern Baptist Convention, to send 40 percent of its church contributions to the state executive secretary for distribution among the various causes which our denomination was supporting. The main geographical area for experimenting in new systems of church financing pointing toward the Cooperative Program seems to have been Western Kentucky, where groups of churches developed cooperative ways of promoting Christian giving according to the three words that had been laid out in the original charter. This seems to have been the first reaching toward the shaping of the Cooperative Program as we now know it.

The first massive denominational endeavor to develop into a systematic way of fund raising became known as the "Seventy-five Million Campaign." Over a brief, stated period of time church members were encouraged to support all Southern Baptist causes according to needs. Southern Baptists pledged $92,630,923.00 to this campaign. While the total amount was never reached, because of the unstable economy following World War I, more money came in to support Baptist causes than in any other equal time in the denomination's history. The total received was $58,591,713.69. And the most significant thing about it was that the groundwork was being laid for the Cooperative Program to be introduced as a permanent system of denominational financing. It has proven to be the soundest system of financing Southern Baptist mission and ministry efforts. A new day had dawned at that point for Southern Baptists' general denominational support.

One of the keys to the success of the Cooperative Program was that the state conventions took the lead in the promotion of stewardship programs in order to seek sufficient funds to support all Baptist causes in those states in the Southern Baptist Convention. A joint commitment was made that Southern Baptist agencies, institutions, and boards would no longer solicit churches directly for funds to finance their causes *if* state conventions would agree that whatever undesignated funds were received through the denominational channels would be shared equitably with the Southern Baptist Convention for support of its own agencies, institutions, and programs.

The word "Cooperative" in the title "Cooperative Program" has come to imply that it is the program of Southern Baptists used to finance their joint endeavors through a common fund. Originally, however, it was used almost as a legal term defining a semicontractual agreement between the Southern Baptist Convention and the several state conventions providing that all funds received in the joint effort would be equitably shared if the Southern Baptist agencies would no longer solicit directly through church budgets. This is the continuing reason why all state conventions should seek diligently to maintain the fifty-fifty division of all undesignated funds with the national body. This was basic in the original planning. While not a formal contractual agreement, it was a fair system approved by both, under which all Baptists work cooperatively. The original working agreement makes it almost mandatory that both parties adhere to the original concept for balance between the Baptist work of the states and the Baptist work of the national body in a constantly equitable manner.

In the present day an acute problem has emerged. Southern Baptist agencies are forbidden to solicit directly from the churches, as mentioned above. But para-church groups and independent schools begun apart from the Convention can and do solicit, and seek to get listed in local church budgets on a sustained basis. These independent institutions sometimes call themselves Southern Baptist, even though they are not related to any Southern Baptist denominational body. For them to have a favored position and be able to do that which Convention institutions are forbidden to do turns the incentive structure upside down. Such imbalance rewards the noncooperating institutions which are not owned and operated by the Convention, and penalizes the institutions which are cooperative and which are owned and operated by the Convention itself.

As it turns out, much of the criticism of Southern Baptist seminaries seems to be initiated by some proponents of the independent seminaries who are seeking to create suspicions against the denomination's institutions so they can raise more funds for their own schools. Unconsciously or consciously, they have taken on the techniques of advertising used for many commercial products over television. They spend more time downgrading competitors than they do in stating the qualities of their own wares. This is one of the most pressing problems Southern Baptists now face, and it produces many unjustified criticisms which have little or no basis in fact.

As it is now, the Cooperative Program is the main line of support for state Baptist conventions and their programs and institutions, as well as for the entire Southern Baptist Convention and its programs. The Cooperative Program is systematic, ongoing, economical, and as long as Baptists tithe will be adequate. It always magnifies giving through the local church. It removes the competition among agencies and the various Baptist bodies who on occasion would vie for the same dollar in contribution. It simplifies bookkeeping. While, like all other systems, it may have a few weaknesses, it is as near to being error free as any system any denomination has ever been able to devise. It should not be sold short or downgraded. Of course, because of its importance and influence, it stands as the first point of open attack by spiritual enemies who would oppose Southern Baptist cooperative endeavors and seek to do injury to our denomination. Fortunately, the Cooperative program has been able to stand the test of many unjustifiable attacks and will continue to do so because of its many undeniable merits.

The time when the Southern Baptist Convention grew to the point of setting up the Cooperative Program in 1925 was the time when Southern Baptists could move away from *soliciting* and change to the historically proper word, *eliciting*. No other denomination plans have had so many strengths and so few weaknesses. *Baptists who practice Cooperative Program giving will support directly and indirectly everything Southern Baptists do.* A part of the funds will go for work nearby. Other parts of the gift will go to the furthermost parts of the world. It should be supported and promoted ardently by every individual Baptist and every Baptist group. Advance comes through exploiting strengths to the fullest in a positive manner. Advance comes through participation, not abdication or criticism.

In the early days of the Cooperative Program, the funds that came to the Southern Baptist Convention were divided strictly on a percentage basis. It was predetermined that approximately 50 percent of all undesignated gifts would go to foreign missions, and approximately 25 percent would go to home missions. This meant that all other SBC agencies and causes would be financed out of the remaining 25 percent, including institutions, commissions, committees, and all special denominational activities. In recent years the funding has been done more on the basis of merit than on fixed percentages. This means that each year the efficiency with which agencies do their work becomes a basis by which recommendations are made for their receipt of funds during the year ahead. Each agency has to justify its requests with a detailed statement of program, stating its intended use before the money is given and committing itself to the highest possible efficiency in the use of appropriations made. In this way, agencies are challenged to do their best, and contributors are assured of maximum efficiency of each dollar given.

The most often-heard criticism of the Cooperative Program is that it tends to be somewhat impersonal. Giving to specific causes at specific times can be rewarding, but giving to all denominational causes simultaneously should be even more so. Giving is not *to* the Cooperative Program but *through* the Cooperative Program for the ministry of Christ around the world. We give to support missions and ministry, witness and teaching, healing of humanity's hurts, and hundreds of other causes which Baptists undertake and believe in. Improvement of techniques and denominational interpretation and promotion perhaps can make giving more personal. Much improvement to this end has been made in remarkable ways in recent years.

In eliciting support for the Cooperative Program, the final use of the funds to be spent among the people served should be stressed more than the system into which the funds flow when given. People are more interested, for example, in hot biscuits than they are in how a kitchen stove is made. They may have some degree of concern for the method, but their major interest is the product produced. The end result needs to be kept in focus. We can learn something from the present advertisements of the telephone company. These messages do not focus on the exchange system and how it operates but on the theme, "Reach Out and Touch"—magnifying the importance of constant person-to-person contact. That is exactly what the Cooperative Program is. It is every Southern Baptist joining with every other Southern Baptist so that together they can "Reach Out and Touch" the world for Jesus Christ.

Figures from 1982 demonstrate that Southern Baptists have adopted an effective and efficient means of financing a worldwide program. During 1982 gifts to the Cooperative Program were $93,344,356. Designated receipts, including such items as missions and education, totaled an additional $80,578,473. These dollars support 3,430 home missionaries, 3,217 foreign missionaries, institutions, and the many agencies and programs that relate to our work for Christ.

Through Cooperative Program giving one helps to make preaching possible in the most remote villages of the world where people have never heard of the name of Jesus. Funds given through the Cooperative Program support orphan children who could go unfed without Baptist concern, compassion, and contributions. Young ministers who will serve in many ways in our churches are studying in seminaries supported through Cooperative Program gifts. Knowing these things makes giving more personal.

Giving to the causes of Christ is a joy of the highest order to every giver. It is now. It always has been, as expressed in the words of Jesus, "It is more blessed to give than to receive" (Acts 20:35).

11

Auxiliary and Other Baptist Groups

To understand Southern Baptists, we need to observe them in their broadest working relationships as well as in the internal structure of the Southern Baptist Convention itself. This leads us, then, into a brief study of Woman's Missionary Union, historical societies, the Baptist World Alliance, the American Bible Society, and other relationships, or lack of them, with Christian bodies around the world.

Woman's Missionary Union

It is generally agreed that the Woman's Missionary Union was begun in 1888 in Baltimore, Maryland, but missionary societies in the South, especially for children, had been in existence since before 1800 for the purposes of missionary education, and promotions of missionary contributions for the support of missionaries were undertaken. It seems to have been in the First Baptist Church of Charleston, South Carolina, where so many other movements were first undertaken, that the first children's society was begun. This time it was under the heading "Juvenile Missionary Educational Society"—primarily in behalf of missions to the Catawba Indians. As the young people studied and gave, they developed a deep personal interest in the cause of missions. And as they grew into adulthood, many ways were open for the men for further missionary leadership positions. But women had not been given the privilege of speaking in most Southern Baptist churches at that time, and they felt unduly handicapped. Such a situation did not lessen their missionary zeal and contributions. In fact, some five hundred different missionary societies had sprung up in the South. Women's groups began to meet together to give mutual

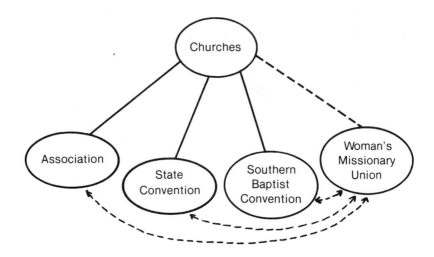

Woman's Missionary Union is an integral part of the denomination but not of the Convention. It is auxiliary to the Convention with an informal relationship and ongoing communication system with the various Baptist bodies (Convention, state conventions, associations) while they carry on their missionary and prayer programs in the churches. Its type of organizational structure cannot mesh with the Convention type; so they function in a cooperative way, but each is separate. Woman's Missionary Union structure is based on the society system. In the chart the solid lines represent an ownership and controlling relationship. The broken lines signify an informal relationship and communication system. In some states and associations the women's work has been brought into direct organized relationship like Sunday School, Church Training, Church Music, and Brotherhood.

support for the common interest they all had in missionary endeavors.

It is sometimes assumed that these first women became interested in missions as adults. The fact is, it came about in the opposite way. Children, deeply interested in missions, refused to lessen their interest and support when they became adults. In many ways they would find outlets and expressions for their zeal for missions. Some of them surrendered for mission service at home and abroad. Others organized in an effort to increase the financial base on which the missionary movement would be funded and thus thrust forward. Having been taught missions in their childhood and youth, the educated and zealous young adult women would not be stifled in their missionary interest and activity. Especially interested were the women who had been taught missions from their youth up, had been enlisted in an intensive prayer effort daily to support the missionaries wherever they were, and in giving sacrificially to their support in every way available to them. At first, the one available way of financial support for most women was very limited. It involved giving what was called "egg money," the small savings they had been able to lay aside from small funds available to them.

One of the true handicaps was that women had not yet been recognized as messengers to the Southern Baptist Convention. Thus they had no privilege of speaking or voting when the Convention was in annual session even when dealing with missions. If anything, this fact increased their zeal and determination. Unfortunately, in many churches, pastors had misunderstood Paul's admonition for silence on the part of women. What had concerned Paul was that the women in pagan temples had shaved their heads, spoken in constant jabber, and enticed men into the pagan rites which we would consider immoral. Paul was most anxious that the general public of that time not mistake the women members of the Christian church with that immoral pagan group, so he insisted that their practices be so different that no passerby could miss seeing drastic differences. Thus he insisted on their silence, long hair, and covered heads for the purpose of making an undeniable distinction. For many years some of our churches, misunderstanding the history, generalized Paul's concern and thought it should be universally applied. They sought to make his concern the prevailing practice in the churches; so women were, therefore, discouraged from speaking in almost all of the local Baptist churches of the land. Even though the Southern Baptist Convention is not a church, it was felt that restrictions placed upon women in churches should apply also at the Convention. Women were not given the privilege of being official messengers for many years lest they be tempted to speak in public.

Women began to attend the Southern Baptist Convention meetings with their husbands. Not being able to speak in Southern Baptist Convention meetings, they began to assemble in separate meetings in nearby church buildings, mostly of other denominations, while the Convention sessions were underway. The theme of their early discussions, of course, was missions. Later this subject became the theme of every year's meeting of the women during Convention time. It still is. Under the leadership of Annie Armstrong, this led to the organization of Woman's Missionary Union in 1888 in Baltimore, although informal meetings had been held by the women long before that time.

The organizational system chosen by the women at that time was the British system of denominational adminstration, namely, the "society system." So they organized into a missionary society. It was not to be a part of the Convention, nor was it subject to Convention actions or directives. Made separate because of the early objection to some Convention messengers being female, the Woman's Missionary Union was set up in an informal relationship to the Convention and designated "Auxiliary to the Southern Baptist Convention."

Fortunately for Southern Baptists, the Woman's Missionary Union made *a very significant policy decision* that caused them to function differently from a true historic society concept. They did not choose to select, send, and support their missionaries separately, as had been done in most true society systems. Instead, they preferred to pass all financial gifts through the regular Convention channels and agencies, through the Foreign and Home Mission Boards to support them in the work assigned to them. Later their prayer efforts came to support state missions as well as home and foreign missions. Today, their gifts are channeled as designated mission gifts through regular denominational channels. This makes them significant supporters of missions of every type through the hundreds of millions of dollars given during their Weeks of Prayer across the years.

It is fortunate the way things developed. The logical thing to have done at the time of founding would have been to set them up as a separate department within the Convention, so that in due time they would function like Sunday Schools or other church-related organizations. History shows, however, that such would have been an unfortunate placement. Had in time they been placed by the side of Sunday School in an institution like the Sunday School Board, not founded until 1891, they could not have been active in the raising of funds for missions, which was one of their main purposes. Although the auxiliary status is sometimes awkward and misunderstood, the women deserve the right to do their work in their own way. And the only question I have ever raised has been whether any organization can be auxiliary to a local church. It is understandable how they could be in an auxiliary relationship to district associations, state conventions, and the Southern Baptist Convention. But can anything be auxiliary to a local church?

At one point it seems that the Woman's Missionary Union is put in a most favored position among Convention agencies by its national president being automatically declared an ex officio member of the Executive Committee of the Southern Baptist Convention. Such is not done for any other organization functioning within local churches like Sunday School, Church Training, Church Music, or Brotherhood. But when one studies history and sees that all WMU gifts are sent through regular denominational channels, then the addition of the president as an ex officio member of that committee seems logical and right. Too, being in an auxiliary status, the Woman's Missionary Union needs to be kept in the closest

possible communication with the Southern Baptist Convention in all of its programs and endeavors.

My appreciation for the zeal for the mission cause of the
women runs deep. After they came into existence and
assumed responsibility for work among the children in
missionary advance, I became a recipient of their endeavors.
As a member of the Sunbeam Band in 1914, before my school
age had arrived, I received my first impressions of a worldwide missionary responsibility on the part of a local church
at the feet of an unmarried member of our church who gave
her life to this young group. She had made this her one major
church responsibility. I was blessed by her teaching under
Woman's Missionary Union which made me aware of the
need for a worldwide witness on the part of each Baptist
congregation. The influence of those teachings still remains
with me and has influenced my actions across the years.

For many years the Woman's Missionary Union directed
the missionary education program for boys as well as girls.
But the women came to the point of feeling that such a
program for boys should be carried on by men instead of
women, especially after the boys had reached their teenage
years. A committee was set up to study this matter and make
recommendations to the Convention according to their find-
ings and best judgment. Having served on that committee I
supported the idea of the transfer, especially for older young
men. When the transfer came, the entire program for boys
over five was placed in the hands of the Brotherhood
Commission so that those boys could have male leadership,
giving them role models in missionary activity. This would
keep the young men from the unconscious feeling that
missions were wholly a woman's responsibility.

There have been two efforts in the last few decades to
assign the Brotherhood Commission, along with its young
people's missionary education programs, to the Sunday
School Board, so this program could take its place by the side
of Sunday School, Church Training, and Church Music, the
other Southern Baptist Convention organizations working
with local churches which across many years have been the
assignment of the Sunday School Board. Each time, however,

the Sunday School Board has discouraged the idea. The problem was that all of its Board programs were designed for men and women, boys and girls. Sunday School Board leaders could hardly see how they could mesh a program for males only into the system under which they had operated for years. It has been the expressed wish of the Southern Baptist Convention that the Sunday School Board correlate its work with that of Woman's Missionary Union in order that more harmony might exist in the local church programs, with no possible grounds for competition between church organizations. For this reason, the Sunday School Board has steered clear of duplicating Woman's Missionary Union programs and activities in its own work. This seemed to be the way the Convention wanted it. But this meant that men and boys would not get proper missionary education and training like the women, unless an agency like the Brother-hood Commission would plan and promote the program which should be as genuinely masculine as the woman's missionary programs were feminine in nature. At the same time, missions would be at the heart of the program because that would be their reason for being. While Woman's Missionary Union is not an integral part of the Southern Baptist Convention, it is a vital part of the denomination.

Historical Societies

Being young, the Southern Baptist Convention for many years had little interest in the knowledge and preservation of its history, especially of local churches. If this important facet were done at all, it was accomplished by persons with a natural interest in historical records and items. The society approach, again, was the only way for history and historical items to be gathered in a systematic way and preserved, as interested individuals organized for the purpose of gathering appropriate historical documents and recording them. These societies sprang up, especially in the older states, usually sponsored by several persons with a burning zeal for the preservation of history. Once the Convention had matured to the point of vibrant interest in historical preservation, it authorized the organization of the Historical Commission in 1951 and funded it to assume leadership in gathering and preserving historical materials. But many state Baptist historical societies had been organized across the years. Those societies had collected important documents and other items which had been placed with them as a trust and, therefore, could not be conveyed to anyone else. So state societies have remained separate and must continue to do so for the preservation of documents entrusted to them. The Historical Commission works with state Baptist historical societies and local church history committees. These groups seek to preserve significant historical materials and to encourage Baptists to study and understand their heritage.

American Bible Society

Because of the deep love Southern Baptists have for the Bible, they have declared support for the American Bible Society, founded in 1816, and its translations of the Bible without interpretation or comment in the many tongues spoken around the world. The Convention has encouraged contributions to this old society located in New York City, which works with similar societies around the world in many significant ways. The American Bible Society's work has been helpful to missionary boards and military units through many translations and distributions of the Bible for many years. The Convention, therefore, encourages the churches to contribute directly to the society in a special emphasis time set into calendars each year. Too, each year at the Convention special recognition is given to the American Bible Society in a resolution because of its special services in the preservation and wide distribution of God's Word.

Baptist World Alliance

In London, England, in 1905, Baptists began regular worldwide meetings on a sustained basis to accomplish certain things which could not be done in any other way. The Alliance is not made up of individual churches but of Baptist bodies who wish to participate in a worldwide fellowship of this sort. Right now well over one hundred Baptist bodies from around the world are represented in the list of Baptist World Alliance members. Each Baptist body can encourage its members to attend the Congress meetings held at five-year intervals in different cities around the world. They meet during the years divisible by five. Work is carried on between the Congress meetings by elected representatives from the many Baptist bodies. This annual meeting is known as the General Council. It does its work according to constitutional provisions given by the full Congress in order that Alliance work might continue uninterrupted between its big meetings.

At first, the main purpose of the Alliance was fellowship only. It moved from that to depth studies by special commissions and study groups dealing with such matters as doctrine, ethics, relationships between Baptist bodies, Baptist similarities, and even Baptist differences. When funds became available, the Baptist World Alliance became a strong influence in worldwide relief work when major disasters occurred anywhere in the world, especially where Baptist missionaries have not been sent by one of the major Baptist bodies who could direct such work in crisis times. Women's work and youth work have been strong in their specific areas within the framework of the Baptist World Alliance for a long time. Men's work came into existence at a more recent time, as did emphasis on Bible teaching and membership training. Evangelism is now a strong emphasis, usually referred to in the Baptist World Alliance as "reconciliation." From both sides of the Iron Curtain representatives have come to the Baptist World Alliance meetings since 1955. Religious freedom is the chief concern for the Alliance around the world. The alliance headquarters are in Washington, D.C. In spite of many differences between Baptist groups, Southern Baptists have benefited greatly by membership in the Baptist World Alliance and its related meetings. The Alliance has benefited also. Most of all, the gospel of the Kingdom of God has been proclaimed.

Relationships with Other Christian Bodies

Southern Baptists are individualists but not isolationists. They like to be themselves, acting on their own convictions, and they are slow to unite organizationally with other groups, even other Baptist groups. It can be remembered that it took two successive years of debating for the Southern Baptist Convention to make up its mind to participate even in the North American Baptist Fellowship, a unit of the Baptist World Alliance operating on the American scene.

Organized connections of any kind are not readily accepted by Southern Baptists. Especially are they not considered "joiners" or supporters of church-unity movements. For that reason Southern Baptists are sometimes referred to as being narrow. This, however, is not true at all. Baptist concepts of salvation, for example, are broader than those of most any denomination in existence. Baptists believe that an individual, any individual, can be redeemed by a simple faith in Christ as Savior, leading to a public declaration of that acceptance of Christ as personal Savior and Redeemer. This doctrine means that there is a total difference in concept from that of many denominations which hold that baptism and the Lord's Supper are integral parts of the salvation experience itself. We believe that the blood of Jesus Christ cleanses "from ALL sin" (see 1 John 1:7), leaving nothing to be cared for in any other way. Baptists would argue that there are redeemed people in all denominations and even among those who have not joined a church of any denomination. It is the Baptist concept that church membership, as important as it might be, is not a part of the redemption process. This illustrates our breadth as a Baptist people.

Many Baptists gladly join in common efforts to defend religious freedom of all people, to regulate and control the sale and use of alcoholic beverages as an intoxicating beverage, and many other moral and ethical causes. But they do not want organizational entanglements regardless of what the issues might be. Of course, a local church does as it wishes in this matter, but the Convention as a whole has sought unity without union. They have not felt that joining into an organizational body to accomplish these things is essential. With this background it can be understood why we have said that Southern Baptists are individualists but not isolationists. Southern Baptists are needed. And they need other believers.

12

Positioning
Southern Baptists

Theologically, Southern Baptists are a grass roots, middle-of-the-road people. Never have they been extreme leftists, nor have they been extreme rightists, in our theological world. But just how are Southern Baptists to be classified?

It seems appropriate, even necessary, to classify Southern Baptists if certain insights are to be gained which are needed to analyze our own denomination adequately. This must be done, however, with the recognition that the same individual Baptist may be conservative in some fields of thought and at the self-same time be looked upon as liberal in other areas. This is one of the things which makes a discussion like this somewhat precarious. Too, just as individuals can be considered conservative in certain areas and liberal in others, the same can be said about individual Baptist churches. Even the Southern Baptist Convention, which is conservative in its theology, is very progressive in its methodology.

I feel definitely that it is worth the risk to point out some facts we need to know and consider before we develop ingrained fears that the Convention is gravitating either to the right or to the left. We hear each of these charges, but can both be true? Is either true? Sometimes a man who talks about "trends" in the Convention has himself shifted either toward a liberal or more fundamental viewpoint. It is quite easy for one to feel that other individuals are the ones who have done the gravitating.

We do know that there are many denominations much more liberal in their theological views than Southern Baptists. A graphic illustration of this came when a book published by Broadman Press was under attack by some Baptists for what they considered a tendency toward "theological liberalism." A copy of that book was placed in the hands of a pastor of another well-known denomination with a request that he evaluate the book's content. After reading it through, he returned the copy with the comment, "I wouldn't worry about that. We have Fundamentalists like that author in our denomination, too." This book, which was considered to be liberal by a number of our people, was considered extremely conservative by this pastor in another denomination. So it goes. Often the liberal or conservative label says more about where the critic stands than where the criticized one is located theologically.

A Fundamentalist theological viewpoint can be just as dangerous to Southern Baptists as a liberal viewpoint would be. Either way, there is extremism. A person can lean backward as well as forward. He is off balance either way he leans. In my view, the ultraconservatives have done the most devastation to our denomination in the past, not the liberals. It needs to be remembered that there have been at least three major efforts to pull our denomination to the extreme right within the last 150 years. One effort was led by a conservative theologian, J. R. Graves, who founded the Landmark Baptist group because he felt that Southern Baptists were in danger of losing their identity. Another was caused by Alexander Campbell in the 1830s when he insisted that baptism be considered essential to salvation, a purely rightist position in the theological world. Southern Baptists have never believed such. Older members of our Baptist life still remember the intense threats brought about by a highly critical preacher in the Southwest named J. Frank Norris. He sustained a movement over a span of years which kept Southern Baptists under constant attack because he felt they were too liberal in theology and practice. In reality, he was too ultraconservative for our denomination. He not only criticized every program of our denomination constantly but kept every denominational officer and leader under relentless attack. When it is remembered that our denomination is built on trust and voluntary cooperation, it is easy to understand how a person, if capable and consistent, can create distrust just by continuously raising certain types of questions and making certain types of offhanded innuendos to reduce confidence.

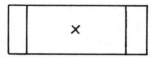

How Democracy Functions

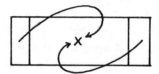

How Criticism Operates

| Ultraliberal | Liberal | Conservative | Ultraconservative |

Broad Spectrum of Christian Bodies in America

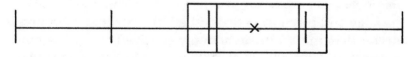

Southern Baptists in Relation
to Other Christian Bodies
in America

The point I'm making is that Southern Baptists might be called conservatives with the little letter c but not conservatives with a capital C. Southern Baptists may be called fundamentalists with a small f, but certainly they are not and have never been Fundamentalists with a capital F. We are attempting to illustrate by the accompanying chart that in the general theological world Baptists are right in the center of things, believing and acting in a conservative manner consistently but refusing to be drawn to the far left or far right. Never have Southern Baptists been extreme in their doctrinal viewpoints as some religious groups are and have been.

Southern Baptists sometimes have a rather disconcerting tendency to interpret doctrines from the limited perspective of their own denomination. They often think only within the framework of where we are as a people in Southern Baptist life and ignore the broad spectrum and general viewpoints of other Christian groups in our nation.

What needs to be seen is that a person who is a conservative in the general religious field can sometimes be looked upon as a liberal within Southern Baptist life. Basically, we are a grass roots, middle-of-the-road denomination resisting ultraconservative positions just as we do liberal positions. Remember, Jesus was much more critical of the Pharisees who were the literalists in his day than he was the Sadducees who were so liberal that they denied the resurrection. He saw more danger in the ultraconservative spirit and attitude than he did in some of the more liberal theological viewpoints of his day. The point I'm making is that ultraconservatism should be avoided just as studiously as liberalism. Sometimes it is more dangerous to us.

Looking at the denomination itself, when is it in its healthiest position? We will see, as illustrated by the chart, that it is when about 10 percent of the messengers to an annual Convention will be looked upon by Southern Baptists themselves as being more progressive than the masses with only a sprinkling of those who might be called liberal theologically. It should be emphasized that it is highly unlikely that there are any "real liberals" in the Southern Baptist Convention. As one of the elements in the chart will show, when Southern Baptists are compared with the total sweep of American Christianity, even those who are toward the left in our denomination are still very close to the center of Christian theology. Real liberals simply cannot fit into the Baptist concept. By the chart you will see that there is likewise a 10 percent group identified at the right who feel that everything is moving too rapidly to the left for them. They are continuously trying to slow things down or pull every movement toward a rightist direction. Some of these seem to consider themselves as being pulled at times by some unseen gravity which they are resisting continuously. It is actually a pull toward center that they feel, because the bulk of our denomination has never been at the extreme end of conservatism.

These two groups of about 10 percent each are the ones who debate every controversial issue that comes up on the floor of the Convention. The 80 percent in the middle, called the "silent middle," are listening intently, and by the ensuing discussions are able to separate truth from error and present a motion that will be generally acceptable to Southern Baptists before the vote is taken. This is a healthy process. It is even a necessary process if democracy is to function. While extremists outside the denomination are to be avoided, those considered extremists within the denomination render an indispensable service to the democratic process. It is a situation that encourages vigorous debate out of which can come correct answers. This process of precipitating debate on major issues is a very welcome and healthy one unless the opposite extremes within the Convention begin to seek to disenfranchise the opposition.

If my observations are correct, the Convention is essentially in the same position in the theological world that it has been over the past several decades. The Convention itself is fairly well locked into a solid position and seeks to make sure that its decisions are correct by encouraging debate on the part of those who have different viewpoints. It is unfortunate that some people do not like to hear debating. To them it seems like an un-Christian arguing. But it needs to be remembered that discussion is the vehicle of change in a democratic process. Each side of an argument ought to be considered seriously in the sincere effort to separate truth from error in the minds of all messengers.

It might be observed that there is an occasional departure of a local church from Southern Baptist Convention life, which any church can do any time unless property deeds and titles are involved. My experience has been that the majority of those churches come back after they have discovered that much of the error was within themselves rather than in the Convention. Unfortunately, when some churches break fellowship with Southern Baptists, they usually do it noisily and with much publicity. Then, when they return, it is usually in silence with the hope that no one will be looking.

Of course, no church "joins" the Southern Baptist Convention. Literally speaking this means, therefore, that it cannot "withdraw" from a Convention it has not joined. It either cooperates or does not cooperate with the Convention. It is just that simple.

Away from the denomination, these churches usually feel an extreme loneliness and suffer from an isolation they have forced upon themselves. Of course, sometimes they may have a justifiable complaint. There is no such thing as a perfect system, even among Southern Baptists. Just as there is no perfect individual, so there is no perfect church. Nor is there a perfect denomination. For that reason, there are some areas in which any denomination or denominational position can be criticized justifiably. The fortunate thing is that even our most ardent supporters in Southern Baptist life feel the liberty to be verbally critical when they see an influence or movement with which they are in disagreement. This is why it is so vitally necessary to have messengers from the Southern Baptist churches from all over the nation who will feel free to enter into these discussions objectively so that the best possible answers can be found and balance maintained.

One church which became upset with Southern Baptists withdrew fellowship in anger and withheld contributions to the Cooperative Program over a period of three years or so. It was exceedingly critical until it found that the Convention was *not* the basis of the problem. The real problem was an unscrupulous pastor. Discovering their situation and realizing what they had done, they began to cooperate more zealously than ever in Southern Baptist life. When asked about their move away and subsequent return their only comment was, "We paid an exceedingly high tuition in the school of experience for the hard lesson we learned."

One of the difficult things for leaders in Southern Baptist denominational life is how to receive and analyze criticism. If an institution or board is properly positioned, it will get letters of criticism from both extreme sides constantly. Instead of trying to convince someone or some institution that his own conservative position is correct, an ultraconservative person usually will condemn the institution publicly for being at the opposite end of the spectrum from himself. Thus, a conservative will tend to call that person or institution liberal. In a similar manner, a person who is liberal in theology will attack that same person or institution by using the label Fundamentalist instead of trying to convince others that his position is correct. This means that criticism is always directed toward the side that is away from the source of the attack. One of the elements in the chart illustrates this principle. The most basic principle of administration for any agency or institution, therefore, is that it must operate at the center of its constituency. A true leader is one with skill who will never identify himself with either extreme group. Insofar as he is able, he will operate near the center of the silent middle. With a healthy 80 percent of the messengers in the silent middle, and with listening ears turned in both directions, more valid answers can be found and positions held.

At times, the Convention has been swept into extremism, most frequently by ultraconservatives. This has brought problems each time. Revisions usually were made the following year or at one of the subsequent Conventions when messengers realized that they had moved away from the center of the constituency too drastically, and they moved back toward center.

It is well that we mention here that generally our denomination is more conservative theologically and socially than many, but inherently progressive in its methodology. So in the final analysis, each messenger can be liberal in certain areas of thinking and conservative or ultraconservative in others. This stands true when the Convention is in session, as some decisions indicate a move in one direction and some in the other. This is why Conventions are sometimes hard to interpret until time has elapsed, and we can look back objectively upon them to consider Convention actions analytically.

Sometimes it is hard to determine where the "middle" is with Southern Baptists. There are certain identifiable characteristics which change as we move. For instance, if one starts at the Atlantic and moves westward, theology gets more conservative. As one moves from the Canadian border to the Gulf of Mexico, stands on social issues become more conservative. As one starts at the Pacific and moves eastward, music gets more conservative. So one can in honesty ask, "Where is the middle?"

Appeals are made frequently for us to defend our agelong principle of "unity in diversity" which is not only vital but absolutely imperative if we are going to preserve our autonomy of local churches. The principles of the priesthood of the believer and the autonomy of the local church force us to keep the church sovereign in all its denominational relationships. The difficulty in maintaining the principle of unity in diversity is that there are certain people who find it difficult to cooperate with those who do not hold views identical to their own. A few times in my memory, when emotions were high, the Convention would take extreme positions only to discover that it had created problems more intense than the ones which existed before. For example, at one time it was agreed that states ought to nominate members of the Committee on Boards from their particular states. A state-by-state caucus would be held on the Convention floor. However, it is an obvious violation of Baptist polity for one group to nominate the members of a committee for another body. In this case, states were determining members of a Convention committee. This action was subsequently corrected.

When everyone sees everything alike, and few or no

objective discussions are heard, invalid decisions are more frequently made. Democracy has its own principles which must be followed, and when these democratic principles are not properly respected, someone will ultimately rise up with an autocratic attitude. He will exercise too much dictatorial-type leadership on his own, which is most disconcerting in a democratic process. This happens in government and religion. In government, anarchies usually arise when democratic processes fail. In a denomination, we simply lose some precious time but usually return to correct gross errors when they have been made. All talk may be considered cheap and tedious by some messengers to a Convention, but discussion is vital and necessary to healthful and mature actions.

The appeal for diversity within unity is a timely one. When we can chuckle at such statements as "The only thing on which any two Baptists will agree is how much the third one ought to give to the Cooperative Program," we can know that the situation is relaxed. When such a relaxed position prevails, arguments will not get personal, and correct answers can be reached without undue loss of time. It is when feelings are intense, people take themselves too seriously, no diversity is allowed, and humor is considered out of order that we get ourselves into trouble. While a few tense moments are inevitable when major controversial issues are up for discussion, it must be kept in mind that there is no place for any degree of intolerance or impatience. If possible, all discussion should be on the basis of the issues at hand and never on personality clashes between individuals or clashes among groups.

A danger point has been reached in a democratic body, whether it be governmental or religious, when one extreme group attacks those personally at the opposite pole from him. Then there is a reciprocal action and attacks come back on the attackers. When the two groups at the extreme ends of the Baptist spectrum attack the "silent middle" and call them compromisers in their effort to force Convention actions, we are approaching a crisis time. If discussions can be kept free, extreme situations will not develop, and the silent middle will continue to be the vast majority of the constituency. The institutions can move forward with confidence.

History shows that when religious groups have reached the point of schism and have broken apart, each side of the division then takes exactly the overall shape of the unit that existed before the division—with extremists on each end within each body. If divisions do come the problems are only intensified by that division of the group. Nothing is settled.

A leader in the past who rose up in Southern Baptist life was brilliant and dynamic, even charismatic. He was not the tongue-speaking kind of leader but was one with unusual skill in leading and influencing the masses of people. He could sway people easily. He led a rightist splinter group to pull away from the Convention because he disagreed with some of the Convention's policies which he considered too liberal. We call it a "splinter" group when such a group does break away because that is actually what it becomes. The splinter soon burns out in a furious flame, while the "huge old log" continues to burn on as it did before. But look what has happened. The splinter group now begins to splinter within itself. It divides into subgroups, and struggles continue. I was in a city preaching some years ago where within a mile and a half radius of the church there were more than a dozen small, struggling churches which had issued from an original split. Each was fighting within itself as well as everyone else. They had been taught to oppose but had never learned the first lesson of thinking affirmatively. They knew what they were against but never learned what they were for. They never learned the first lessons of cooperation. Therefore, all they knew was division. And the way that movement continuously splintered ought to be a lesson to us all.

What the Southern Baptist Convention seeks to practice is theo-democracy, which is quite different in spirit from a pure democracy. It operates in a different spirit as well as manner and seeks answers which it feels are God's solutions to the problems, rather than our own personal opinions. We all know that democracy can at times be selfish and thoughtless. Theo-democracy never gets that way, because it is seeking to do the will of God directly at all times. A theo-democracy is

God-guided, while a pure democracy can be taken over by groups who have special interests. Theo-democracy produces more light than heat, and people are not nearly as apt to get overexcited when they are trying to ascertain the divine purpose than when they are trying to defend or promote their own personal prejudices. Theo-democracy produces calmer business meetings and more permanent answers.

A president of a Convention is forced to operate at the center of his constituency and not show favoritism to any particular minority group—or even majority group. *Robert's Rules of Order* has been adopted as the Convention's parliamentary guide to forbid unbalanced presentations or lopsided arguments. The presiding officer is required to be fair always. Any time he appears to lean to the one side or the other, his actions will be considered unfortunate. Perhaps the most difficult thing for any leader of the Convention or an institution within it is to get all the facts out to the people before a vote is taken. Regardless of the hard work put forth, it takes a long time to get the message out to the people who are to do the voting. As hard as it might be, people need as many clear facts as possible in order to cast their ballots intelligently.

During my tenure as chief administrative officer at one of Southern Baptists' largest agencies, it was my policy to deal with every criticism that came in, regardless of source. We tried to deal with all correspondence objectively and analytically and learn from it. What we had to learn by experience was that people are ten times more apt to criticize than they are to compliment. So when the letters are 50-50 in ratio, against and for the way things are being done, an institution is to be complimented. When one receives 10 percent compliments and 80 percent critical letters, the public is ordinarily 50-50 in opinion. Any time all of our criticism would start coming from one side, we realized that we had veered from the center of the constituency and needed some readjusting. Dealing with criticism objectively demands a certain type of person, one who is capable of taking criticism objectively rather than personally. It is difficult to administer an institution unless one is able to handle criticism objectively.

In this chapter, while I have dealt with observations growing out of years of experience at the center of the democratic process of our Baptist situation, I have sought to draw analogies and illustrate principles that can become vital parts of any democratic decision-making process. Tremendous patience is required for denominational leaders to maintain composure. Constant changes are being made within the denomination because constant alterations are being made in the world situation around us. All of these situations force an administrative leader of an agency to evaluate changes in the light of current facts and truths. Facts are those things which are constantly changing. Truth is that which is eternal. So, while certain changes do have to be made, those changes have to be made in the framework of unchangeable truths that can never be altered. It is this delineation between fact and truth which remains a constant concern of any effective denominational leader or executive.

Before we close this chapter, there is another item we need to analyze. It will seek to locate Southern Baptists in relation to other Christian bodies in America by use of the chart which we have given. Let us analyze it a moment. A lone line has been given to illustrate the broad and diverse range of Christian groups.

Let us make this sort of approach. At the left end of the long structure of American Christian groups we will identify the liberal religious groups. They will be the ones we refer to generally as extreme leftists, whoever they might be by name. Then at the right end of the line, identify the exact opposite. They are the ultralegalists and ultraliteralists, even ultra-Fundamentalists, by whatever name they might be called. Now, let us ask ourselves where Southern Baptists fall in this broad spectrum of American Christian groups. How would you identify and where would you put Southern Baptists?

We do know that there are a number of denominations to the left of Southern Baptists. They are the liberals who question the authority of the Bible, the deity of Christ, the reality of heaven. They deal with sin and salvation and even the existence of God rather loosely and carelessly as though they were fantasies. The intensity of these liberal views increases as the line flows leftward. And the same is true on the line at the right of center. There are some denominations much more literalistic than Southern Baptists. For instance, there are those who believe that baptism is essential to salvation, taking literally "be baptized . . . for the remission of sins" (Acts 2:38), a position Southern Baptists have never held. Also there are those who believe that the elements of the Lord's Supper actually, literally become the body and blood of Christ, taking literally the statement "this is my body" (1 Cor. 11:24) which Baptists have always taken figuratively. These two positions, along with others, are too much to the right for us. Baptists discourage Phariseeism and extreme Fundamentalism more for their bad spirit than for the content of their beliefs, even though we feel their beliefs are extreme.

In my own half century of active service among Southern Baptists, I have come to believe that we can position Southern Baptists correctly if we locate them very near the theological center as I have shown on the chart. We can position our denomination among the other Christian groups of the land if we superimpose the element in the chart showing the nature of a democratic process near the center of the horizontal line illustrating the religious spectrum of the nation. Our denominational chart would show about 2 to 5 percent of our membership at the left of most Baptists and 2 to 5 percent at the other end to the right. In this way we can properly view Southern Baptists in relationship with others. You will observe that this chart correctly places all of us close to the center. We are not liberals, but we are not Fundamentalists either.

Seeing this point clearly would remove fears that the Convention has a tendency to shift either toward liberalism or conservatism. Neither is the case. Ours is a solidly based denomination and will remain so, while some individual Baptists and even churches may feel occasionally that the Convention is shifting or has shifted its stance. What is happening most of the time is that the critics are more apt to have shifted their own personal positions and have, therefore, come to feel instead that the Convention has altered its historic stance. The Convention and denomination are well-placed and stable.

13

Areas Needing Constant Attention or Improvement

Due to the rather complex nature of Southern Baptist polity, it is amazing that relationships have been so excellent between churches, Baptist bodies, areas, and agencies, as the denomination has grown larger and expanded in territory. In the family of religious denominations our system of operation is totally different from any other religious group. No wonder others have difficulty at times understanding us. There are times when we wonder if we are not a puzzle to ourselves because of the fact that our polity is so different and at times complex.

In the light of the above, it is amazing that there are so few areas which need improvement or correction. There are also, though, several other areas which need constant attention lest some agency or unit wander into an area of assignment rightfully belonging to someone else. In my many years of operation at the heart of Southern Baptist life, I have known only a few times when an agency or a committee made what I would consider a wrong move knowingly. Because of subsequent changes in denominational procedures, that type of violation now seems highly unlikely if not impossible. An agency must get Convention approval now before it moves into any area in which it has not previously functioned or been given a specific assignment. Long ago there seems to have been a tendency for committees to push to become commissions and commissions to push to become boards. At times there have been movements in that direction, without specific assignment. We do not see that now. The areas which currently seem to me to be the ones needing constant self-surveillance or a few specific improvements are:

1. Some district Baptist associations in the denomination insist on nominating persons for membership on executive

boards of state conventions. Such an action, however, is a trend toward a hierarchical structure and should be discouraged. This should be seen as a gross violation of Baptist polity, because each Baptist body is autonomous and should nominate and elect its own officers. A Baptist association should nominate and elect its own officers. A state Baptist convention, even though it may want to have an executive board member from each Baptist association within that state should nominate and elect its own executive board members. The same would hold true of the Southern Baptist Convention and the election of members to the Executive Committee, even though I have never known of a state convention which has sought that privilege. For autonomous bodies to remain autonomous, they must nominate and elect their own officers as a matter of ongoing policy. For any Baptist body to nominate officers of another Baptist body would be comparable to one Baptist church wanting to serve as a pulpit committee for another Baptist church somewhere in the area. This is a point needing constant alertness, and in a few places where the practice is now being carried out, there is a need for correction.

2. In every area of denominational life, more laypersons need to be elected to high positions in Baptist leadership. The vast majority of Baptists are laypersons, and this fact should be recognized when officers are being nominated and elected. Many capable laypersons are skilled to serve in high positions, such as the presidency of the Southern Baptist Convention. We have to note with regret, however, that only three laymen have been elected to the presidency of our Convention within the past fifty years. While this is not precisely a matter of polity, it is a violation of principle which needs attention and correction, lest cleavages be produced in the coming years between ministers and laypersons. Correction will be easier now than later. It will be simpler to prevent than to try to correct after such tensions have occurred.

3. Continuous caution should be exercised by the Sunday School Board lest its sheer size unwittingly create problems for some of the smaller agencies, commissions, and committees. I know that this problem arose a few times when I was

the chief administrative officer of the Sunday School Board, and it did so without my knowledge at the time of occurrence. We were somewhat like the pilots in the Pacific Northwest a number of years ago. For months strange things had been happening on the ground in that part of our nation. Car windshields would suddenly pop out from their frames for no apparent reason. Plate glass windows in stores would seemingly explode. It was soon discovered that this was being caused when planes high above would break through the sound barrier when the plane's nose was pointed toward the ground, creating a powerful sonic boom Earthward. The pilot was flying along intently at great speed and high altitude, totally unaware that he was creating problems for others. When this does occur, the Board needs to know what the problem is so immediate correction can be sought. I recall one problem regarding funding which existed between the Historical Commission and the Sunday School Board for quite some time before it was called to my attention. The Board was set up to serve the denomination and has an ongoing obligation to every area of Baptist life.

4. All Baptist agencies and institutions need to plan a more intense orientation period and program for their newly-elected board members (trustees), including a study of the Southern Baptist Convention charter, constitution, and bylaws, as well as the same documents for the agency which they are to serve. Because Baptists do things differently in different areas, the content in these extremely important documents needs to be clearly understood by all trustees who serve the denomination in any official capacity. Otherwise, it would be only natural that they use methods appropriate in an area they have served before or of secular business management with which they might be more familiar. In doing so they will miss the thrust of their specifically-assigned Baptist duties which are quite different in nature and approach from other institutions.

While all agencies face this problem in some degree, it is the Southern Baptist Convention's Executive Committee which has the most acute difficulty at this point. The Convention seeks the most skilled as well as the most experienced persons from Baptist leadership the nation over to serve on this important committee and should. This means, however, that many of them have served previously on executive boards of state Baptist conventions and have now come to serve on the Southern Baptist Convention's Executive Committee without realizing the organizational differences between these two bodies. It is only natural that when they move from their past position in a state convention to serve on the Executive Committee of the Convention that they would function in the same way they have operated in the past unless they see the differences. The Southern Baptist Convention's Executive Committee is quite different in organization, approach, and relationship from the executive boards of state conventions. To prevent errors from being made in this regard, a more intense orientation period for new members is necessary. In a lesser degree, the same need exists for all Baptist agencies.

5. Local churches should insist that all Woman's Missionary Union officers in a local church be elected by the church they are to serve. Some churches do not elect Woman's Missionary Union officers, even though the organization functions with and among their own church members. While the WMU can rightly be auxiliary to the Southern Baptist Convention, state conventions, and associations, there is no way theologically or organizationally in which it can be auxiliary to a local church. It is either an integral part of the church, or it is separate from it. It must be a part of it to be properly related to it. Even if a separate nominating committee must be set up for that purpose, all leading officers who serve organizations within a church need to be elected by the church in which they will render service. The sovereignty of each church seems to demand this procedure as a matter of policy.

6. Continuous caution needs to be exercised to assure that Cooperative Program Funds are not used for merchandising curriculum materials—which type of denominational service has always carried its own weight by the sale of its own products. If a church's gifts through the Cooperative Program were to be used in the manufacturing of commodities

for distribution back to the churches, those commodities should be presented to the churches without cost. The churches would have already paid for the product by their gifts of money with which the manufacturing was done. This payment has been made out of the mission side of the local church budget by a contribution. If an agency of the denomination were to receive Cooperative Program funds and then use those same funds to manufacture commodities to be sold back to the churches which have made the contribution in the first place, then that Baptist agency would have received funds from both sides of that church's budget. Such would be unfair both to the church and to the Cooperative Program. Payment would have been made out of the local expense side of a church budget by purchases and the mission side of the budget by contribution. Such should be studiously forbidden for the sake of fairness to the churches and to prevent unwanted criticisms against the Cooperative Program.

7. Because the Sunday School, Church Training, Church Music, Woman's Missionary Union, and Brotherhood all relate to kindred organizations within the churches, these five units of work are different and need to have special consideration when it comes to correlation and coordination. Their problems of relating to similar groups within the various state conventions and associations as well as churches are peculiar to themselves. The Southern Baptist Convention would do well to look again at its own process of correlation and ask itself again whether priority should be given to these five organizations as they relate to other Southern Baptist Convention agencies within the Inter-Agency Council, or whether it would be more important that they relate more closely to the kindred organizations within the states and associations in the correlation process. One of these approaches has to take priority over the other.

Until the late 1950s, priority was always given to the correlating process in these five areas with states and associations, each working in its respective areas. For example, all Sunday School secretaries and workers in all bodies would work on the Sunday School program; all Church Training secretaries and workers would work on the Church Training program. Such a procedure would be followed until each of these five church organizations had expressed a strong voice at every level in the development of their own programs from the ground up.

Since the latter 1950s, priority has been given to correlation within the Inter-Agency Council of the Southern Baptist Convention, sometimes making the states and associations feel that they were either coerced, or were being handed, a pre-planned program which they had not helped develop. Now that adequate time has passed since the 1950s, these two approaches can be compared and contrasted adequately to see which is the better way. At least a way needs to be found whereby the state conventions and district associations can be brought into the overall planning process at an earlier point.

8. Checks and balances are needed in a democratic process and are provided in our denomination by the balances required between district Baptist associations, state Baptist conventions (or general associations), and the Southern Baptist Convention. Competition between agencies in any of the bodies, therefore, is not required and should be studiously avoided lest it become counterproductive.

9. No agency's authorities can ever exceed those of the Convention itself. No department or subcommittee can possess more authority than the body which has set it up. At times, I have seen violations or attempted violations at this point.

10. Just because the Sunday School Board does not receive Cooperative Program funds does not mean that it is not an integral part of the Convention in every way. It is controlled by the Convention through trustees elected by that body. *The Cooperative Program is for support, not controls.* Controls are through trustees. The Sunday School Board operates under trustees just like all other agencies, and therefore has exactly the same sort of controlled operation that all other agencies experience. Already we have given an explanation as to why the Sunday School Board does not receive Cooperative Program funds. The Sunday School Board is not in a priv-

ileged position. Its obligations to the entire denomination are felt deeply, and must remain that way. When all is said and done, it is a service organization, not a merchandising venture.

11. State Baptist conventions often reduce their percentages sent on to the Cooperative Program funds of the national body when they feel themselves in a financial bind within their own state. On two different occasions in my young years, I served on two different state executive boards where this was done deliberately to ease our own financial pressures. Frankly, I was not aware of the historic working agreement between the state convention and the Southern Baptist Convention, or what I was doing to Southern Baptist causes when I voted for a larger amount to be kept for use within the state. A fair percentage of division for the Cooperative Program funds in the more developed state conventions is fifty-fifty, the agreement worked out in 1925 when the Cooperative Program was first established. That should be considered the norm and practiced rigidly by all of the older state conventions. Of course, no one would expect a new struggling state convention to reach that percentage until it had had opportunity for more development and growth. Even then, the percentage should increase some each year.

12. Southern Baptist work is spiritual in nature and emphasis. All agencies must keep in mind constantly that while good business and organizational procedures are to be understood and respected, that Southern Baptists do not exist for the purpose of carrying on efficient business enterprises. Southern Baptists work in the spiritual realm, and this is the emphasis which must always keep the ascendency. While each agency will studiously guard against carelessness, mismanagement, and waste, if the situation comes down to the place where it must choose between the spiritual and commercial, the spiritual should always take priority. Financial or business mistakes can be corrected and overcome, in due time. A failure to keep the spiritual emphasis in the forefront of a Baptist agency or institution can be lasting and lead workers into a misplaced emphasis on their own

work, meaning they will miss the basic spiritual purposes of their assignment. The spiritual emphasis must always have priority in every area of Southern Baptist life with every agency and institution.

13. The day will come when the Southern Baptist Convention is going to have to face up to the existence of certain independent parachurch groups and institutions which have sprung up calling themselves Southern Baptist institutions, especially in theological education—even though their charters have not been approved by the Convention, their trustees are not elected by the Convention, and reports are not made to the Convention.

While Baptists under our polity cannot forbid the existence or support of independently operated theological institutions, I personally feel that the Convention should make it known widely that these institutions are not Southern Baptist Convention institutions so churches will understand what they are supporting when these institutions petition local churches to be put in their budgets for ongoing financial support.

The incentive structure is upside down when nonowned and noncontrolled theological schools can solicit local churches for budgeted funds and our own theological schools cannot. The day may come, regretfully, when our own theological schools will have to be given the same privilege in order to compete. Such would be disruptive to the Cooperative Program but may be forced upon us as a Convention if the present trend continues.

14. Certain critics of the Cooperative Program feel that it violates their freedom and coerces them, as well as their local churches, by not allowing withholding from certain causes with which they are not in personal agreement. The criticism might be valid if there were no provision for designated giving already provided. In the present plan, every penny given to Baptist causes, or causes approved by the Convention, goes to the cause or causes designated without even withholding overhead costs. So there is an option already open for people who wish to specify use. If a provision for withholding from certain cooperative causes were approved,

then there would be two systems of designated giving in operation—one positive and one negative. And persons desiring a unified system of giving would have none provided for them. They have rights, too. This is a proposal argued out and settled many decades ago.

To ask the privilege of withholding funds from certain causes supported through the Cooperative program shows a basic misunderstanding of Baptist polity itself. Contributions are not for coercion or control. Trustees are for that. Contributions are for support.

If designation were taken to the extreme, every church in the Convention would end up with endless designations because no local church has unanimous support of every member in every phase of its own work. The genius of the Cooperative Program is that it makes provision for agencies on the basis of need. Every program of every agency has been approved by the Convention and has had its needs evaluated in advance.

Another aspect that many people overlook is that once money is given to a church it is no longer theirs individually. At that point, the congregation determines its use. The same principle applies to the Southern Baptist Convention with undesignated funds placed in its hands. The body of messengers are to determine the best usage. Such is done when budgets are built.

The positive provision for churches and individuals to designate whatever gifts they choose to certain specified causes is necessary. It must be continued.

15. Careful attention, if not correction, needs to be given to the voting imbalance in the Inter-Agency Council of the Southern Baptist Convention. When it was set up on recommendation of the Survey Committee in the later 1950s, each agency was given three votes. At the time this sounded democratic and fair.

The way it worked out in implementation, however, was exactly opposite. The five organizations which operate in local churches are the Sunday School, Church Training, Church Music, Woman's Missionary Union, and the Brotherhood. The voting allocation of the Inter-Agency Council gave the Woman's Missionary Union and the Brotherhood twice the voting strength of Sunday School, Church Training, and Church Music combined, making true correlation almost impossible. This was brought about by virtue of the fact that voting was put on an agency basis rather than a church organization or church program basis, and the majority of the people were virtually disenfranchised in the correlation process. While some improvements were made later by the setting up of subcommittee structures, the basic inequity still remains. It was the desire for correlation of church organizations which caused the Convention to set up the Survey Committee in the first place. In many ways the system provided complicated the process rather than correcting it.

16. It is necessary that state Baptist conventions exercise great care when they start new institutions to make sure that the trustees are elected by and are accountable to the state convention in its annual sessions. Several of the older state conventions have colleges which were set up under a self-perpetuating board of trustees in which the trustees name other trustees when vacancies occur. In almost every instance the institutions with self-perpetuating boards have created difficulties for the state conventions involved because they tend to move farther and farther away from the people and tend to disregard any relationships to the convention itself. Seldom, if ever, has this estrangement developed when the institution's trustees were directly accountable to the messengers from the churches.

17. The only Southern Baptist Convention institution begun under the old society system with a self-perpetuating board of trustees is The Southern Baptist Theological Seminary. No other method was available for it to begin. It operated that way for many years, with the Convention nominating twice or three times as many trustees as there were vacancies. Then the trustees would select the ones they preferred from that list. Such an arrangement was discontinued a number of years ago when the seminary contracted with the Convention that the trustees elected by the Convention would be the ones to serve. That is the way it is done now. Because of some very significant advantages in the old

charter which would be lost if the charter were changed in any way, the Convention has never requested the privilege of rewriting the charter fully, committing the institution to the present system of Convention operation in the new charter. It would be well, however, if the trustees themselves would periodically review the old charter and again ask whether the institution would gain more by revising its old charter than by retaining the present one. The time will likely come when more benefits can come through revision than through retention, but the trustees of the institution should be the ones to sense that timing and take action accordingly.

18. The same principle should apply to the election of trustees for SBC agencies which is used by local churches in the election of messengers to annual sessions of the convention. Long ago the churches abandoned the "delegate" idea in which the representatives were chosen to attend and were sent with preconceived ideas, if not instructions, on how they were to vote on certain issues. They were called *delegates* because they were delegated in advance to represent specific viewpoints, even before they knew how the motions would be worded. Never could one change an emphasis or moderate an idea because he was instructed before going, before knowing what the facts of the case really were. Under that system no valid agreements could ever be reached. Today, if a representative is instructed in advance he should, in theory at least, be rejected as a representative from that church because there is no place in the Convention today for delegates. Messengers are uninstructed representatives sent from churches to find the best Christian ways of doing things together as Baptists.

If the above principle applies to the selection and actions of trustees, we are in good shape. But there are occasional violations of this principle, and it always brings unfortunate results. If an extreme group rises up and organizes to elect certain persons to champion a certain viewpoint, an impossible impasse has already been created. Persons elected under such a condition will learn many facts after their election as trustees, but if they do not continuously represent the uncompromising viewpoint which elected them, they are looked upon by their peers as turncoats or traitors. If they don't shift positions, knowing what they now know, they will have guilty consciences or always vote on the losing side. The majority of Southern Baptists are not extremists, so these trustees will end up either disillusioned or embittered, either of which is unfortunate. It is far better in Baptist life to select the best trustees available and leave it to them to work and pray together until solutions can be found which can be conscientiously supported by all. To try to commit trustees in advance of election to certain persons or ideas is un-Baptistic historically.

14

Anchored to the Past but Gearing for the Future

Years ago when I was a young pastor in a college town, it was my privilege to have Dr. George W. Truett, perhaps our most renowned Southern Baptist preacher ever, to preach several times from my pulpit. His messages were always crisp, current, and challenging, as well as eloquent, and many emphases he stressed during that week are still crystal clear to me. One dealt with a conversation he had with his mother when he was a teenager. She was expressing her anxiety that her son get a good education so he would not have to work slavishly like she and her North Carolina mountain husband had been forced to do all of their lives just to make a living. This sturdy mountain woman had been forced to labor from early morning until well after dark all of her years. Dr. Truett's youthful reply to her revealed his wisdom even in those early days. He said, "Mother, I don't want to appear to be correcting you. But you must know that the purpose of education is not to teach one how to get out of work. Instead, it is to teach one how to accomplish much more with the same amount of effort." So it is in the fields of organization and polity. These two seem closely related.

When our denomination was young and small, our forefathers did not have to worry much about keeping their organization up-to-date. With only a few people working together, communication and unity of effort were easy. Everything was visible and uncomplicated. Not any more. With vast worldwide denominational enterprises now necessary, involving hundreds of professions of people doing complex jobs in interrelated fashion, everything must be long-range and spelled out in detail. Each function must operate wth clocklike precision. But this very situation can be our very undoing, unless we give constant attention to the way we do things, the spirit in which everything must be done, and how it all fits together. Good organization is imperative, but the very nature of organization, as well as purpose, in a Christian body is quite different from that ordinarily seen in the business or secular world. The dog-eat-dog jungle theory of the secular world has no place in a religious body or organization at any level or in any relationship.

Special Leadership Ability Required

A key word in the business world is *management*. The person in charge works with his group of people to see that the optimum level of accomplishments is reached in productivity and achievement by a relentless human push toward efficiency. It is at this point that the difference begins to show between a Christian enterprise and the secular world. More true leadership skills are required of Christian leaders than secular ones.

Every large institution or organization must have an organization chart so each can understand how each job relates to other jobs. Workers then can relate themselves to each other in doing the work which they are employed to do. In the secular world we often see these charts indicating that people are managing people. Not so in Christian organizations. In the Christian realm supervisors supervise jobs, manage work loads, and administer budgets, but at the selfsame time they must *lead* people. In the realm of the spiritual there must always be leadership manifested because in spiritual realms no person can be driven.

Religious leaders must have the highest regard and even love for the people with whom they work daily. And they will be on hand to help personally when things go wrong and assistance is needed. In the secular realm we may not only see efforts to manage people instead of the jobs, but oftentimes when things do go wrong in a secular business the worker may be abandoned, personally blamed, and even terminated, even though he may not be the one responsible for the failure. In a Christian institution the immediate supervisor, who has delegated his job to his helpers, will be right there himself to assist when and as needed. Even though certain tasks can be delegated, it is still the supervisor's personal responsibility to see that the job gets done. Therefore, he delegates tasks to others, but he has an obligation to both workers and the work to serve in a Christian spirit as well as to lead with Christian diligence.

There are certain terms we must not confuse when this aspect of Christian business operation is under discussion. We must make a clear-cut distinction between management and manipulation. The management of jobs may be necessary to get the job done. Manipulation however, is never excusable. It is the moving about of people without feeling, like checkers, for the benefit of the supervisor. True Christian "management" is the assignment and shifting of work loads to the workers so that no one will be overburdened and that all jobs can be carried on in synchronization and fairness to achieve the highest levels possible. While management may be a necessary term in reference to jobs, we should always use *leadership* as the term in relationship to people. This word involves spirit as well as skills, sympathy for the workers as well as the human effort to get the job done, and availability on short notice when personal assistance is needed by any worker.

In a Christian institution we might get the correct concept presented in a better way by taking an organizational chart and laying it on its side instead of viewing it from top to bottom. In its upright position it usually represents the flow of authority by which the work is to be done, showing how jobs related to jobs and positions relate to positions. Turned sideways, however, it looks more like a football play which a coach has drawn on a chalkboard. It shows how people relate to people in a team spirit as the individuals become one larger working unit—each assisting the other. By this approach we can see that persons in responsible positions of leadership will be playing the game right with the others— leading and inspiring in every effort, with no one left out or counted unimportant. All are players on the same team, even the managers and supervisors. As in athletics, only when individuals are meshed into full team play, is there a chance for a championship. It is easy in the secular world to look at a normal upright business organization chart and assume that the persons at the top are the really important ones, and that the persons immediately under them are a bit less important. This process gets to be tragic if the same logic and direction holds until we come to the bottom of the chart and assume that the people located there are of little value because they are at the bottom of the organization chart and seem, therefore, to be of least worth. What tragedy when such an assumption is made! This unwholesome attitude forces labor unions. Gradation in the organizational chart may apply to jobs, because some jobs are more important than others, requiring variations in salary according to the educational preparation required and the weight of the load to be carried daily. But the same principle does not hold with people.

No lessons of my childhood were drilled more into me by my schoolteacher mother than the two statements "There is no such thing as an unimportant person" and "Any job that is honest is honorable." My years of experience have proved the truth and worth of each statement.

The person filling the most menial job in a Christian institution is just as important as the one filling the highest post. Jobs may be rated but not the people who fill them. They are all of infinite worth in the sight of God and should be equally respected in the attitudes of Christian leaders. They deserve the highest respect and the fairest of treatment regardless of the place they hold in the organizational chart. We repeat, jobs may be rated high and low, but not people.

While Southern Baptists must organize well to do their best work with the least of human effort, and give the best accountability for the expenditure of God's money, the importance of the persons filling the jobs should never be minimized in any way at any time. *Organize jobs but lead people.* That should be our motto.

Biblical Approach Necessary

At the outset I mentioned that theology must come into play in the development of Southern Baptist polity, indeed in the organizational development of any denomination. At that time, I cited two of the principle doctrines which help give shape to our polity as being: (1) *the sovereignty of the local church*, and (2) *the priesthood of the individual believer.* The first of these dealt with the rightful place of the local church in Southern Baptist life, it being the most important organizational unit, always to be indicated as being at the top of a Baptist organization chart. The other statement stresses the *soul freedom of man* which completely forbids coercion in matters of religion at any level, or in any area. The first forces autonomy of the local church. The other forces voluntarism and soul freedom in a local church and in every area of the denomination's life and work.

There are other doctrines of our faith set forth in *The Baptist Faith and Message* adopted by the Southern Baptist Convention as an expression and interpretation of our basic denominational beliefs which also affect Baptist polity in a very real way.

The statement on *The Scriptures* identifies the Holy Bible as the "Supreme standard by which all human conduct, creeds, and religious opinions should be tried." The spirit of love and fellowship among persons is important, as well as the high moral and ethical standards required of all Christians. A religious organization has no excuse to do its work shoddily or carelessly with the feeling that because it is God's business, God will see us through in spite of the careless, haphazard way we might do our work. The opposite emphasis should be given, that because it is a religious organization or institution, its work should be done in the most careful and capable way humanly possible. No work is as important as God's work.

The *Doctrine of Man* demands that employees and customers always be looked upon as being of divine worth, as well as the people to whom we are to minister on the field as people of our denomination. Everybody is really somebody, made in the image of God, to be treated with respect and courtesy.

A good philosophy for a religious institution to follow is: "God created all mankind in his own image and has a divine purpose in every life. As Christians we can do no less than to help each individual discover what that divine purpose is, and help him/her achieve it to the highest level of that potential." This principle holds not only with those on the inside of the denomination or its institutions, but also for all workers outside the Christian vocation.

The *Evangelism and Missions* statement gives meaning and purpose to everything we do in our denomination. The statement on *Education* requires a constant process of training and enlightenment. The statement on *Cooperation* is vital in our polity, as well as in the statement on *The Christian and Social Order,* and *Religion and Liberty.*

The entire statement of faith bears in a direct or indirect way on some aspect of Baptist polity. This emphasizes the importance of the *Scriptures* in the shaping of our methodology and organization, as well as our attitudes and relationships toward people.

Spiritual Motivation Imperative

We have said much about organization, leadership, and system in these discussions. Now we must stress motivation. Without it nothing moves. But what brings motivation about? How can we assure ourselves that there will be sustained energy and guidance while the job is being done? In the world of business, motivation is still a puzzle with solutions constantly being sought. It is quite different in the Christian realm with Christian people and individuals in institutions who know God and are seeking to do his will through his divine power. Spiritual workers who are empowered by the Spirit of God are like players on an athletic team who constantly "play above their heads." That term is used often when it seems that basketball players, for example, cannot miss the basket.

Just how influential Christianity is in producing dynamic motivation was shown some years ago when one of America's chief authorities in the field of organizations accepted our invitation to lead one of our training weeks at the Sunday School Board in Nashville. Although he had not accepted field engagements for quite a number of years, he scheduled ours. His explanation was that he wanted to study the influence of Christianity on motivation, by holding conferences with our employees. It had been reported to him by other consultants that Sunday School Board workers were some of the most highly motivated employees they had seen in the entire country. He felt it must be due to some special religious experiences or drives within the workers because of their Christian convictions and commitments. He was right.

Theologically we refer to this "wisdom and power" in Christian workers as being the leadership of the Holy Spirit. Truly it is. He is working within willing Christians, motivating each one to do his job well. Without such motivation in the areas of knowledge and strength, every Christian task would come up lacking. In 1947, my wife and I made our first overseas flight en route to the Baptist World Alliance meeting in Copenhagen. It was also our first journey on a four-motor plane. Soon after we took off from New York, I turned to her with the comment that I did not believe I had ever experienced such a pleasant plane ride. But when we got about one-third across the Atlantic, we encountered an unexpected but severe storm. At the height of the storm's turbulence, a motor died just outside our window. It became necessary immediately to divert the plane to Gander, Newfoundland, for urgent motor repairs. Yet the handling procedure was complicated by a low cloud ceiling of almost zero. Shortwave radios had not been developed at that time to guide planes mechanically to a safe landing. As we were being jostled all over the sky with one motor dead while trying to locate the landing strip, I turned to my wife with the comment, "This is the heaviest thing I ever tried to hold up from the top in all of my days." How different it was from the first few hours of that same flight! The first time the plane was carrying me. Now it seemed that I was having to carry it. What a difference! The contrast was staggering, although I was seated on the same plane and in the same seat.

Where is there a church worker anywhere who has not experienced feelings kindred to this from time to time? When the work of the church is being undertaken alone, it is a burdening routine. When the Holy Spirit carries the work and us, it becomes a joy.

This brings us to some basic truths we would like to underscore and shout from the housetop. Never is there enough human skill or strength to do God's work anywhere at any level without God's leading power. Human skills are never good enough to guarantee achievements in the spiritual realm. We must never forget that even though it was urgent to get the Good News of the risen Christ out to the world immediately after our Lord's resurrection, that the disciples were ordered to "tarry . . . in Jerusalem" until they had been filled with power by the Holy Spirit "from on high" (Luke 24:49) before their undertaking in world conquest would begin. To move without that divine power would mean they would fall flat on their faces in utter defeat at the very outset.

Things have not changed. The disciples back then knew Jesus well. They had lived with him daily for three years. They had trusted their lives to his salvation and leadership. They had sat at his feet time after time ardently drinking in his magnificent teachings. They could quote key phrases word-for-word and enunciate his philosophy as well as his theology. But for them to undertake the gigantic task of winning the world without the infilling of divine power was unthinkable. Not only did there have to be an infilling before they left but a constant refilling of that power while the work was under way. No human genius operating alone was adequate for such an assignment. Divine presence and daily power were imperative. Still, there is one indelible lesson for us given in it all. When God's finger points the way for us, his hand and all of heaven's power will help us move in the direction he has ordained to do the things he has instructed. The potential is limitless when we move in divine strength and wisdom. Energy expended must be constantly replenished. Human wisdom when it reaches its limits must receive more and special revelations. When the human spirit seems to be at the point of breaking, God's encouragement will cause it to engage in a period of rejoicing. As long as the disciples were full of themselves, there was no possible way for them to be filled with the Spirit of God. So a spiritual experience of deep nature had to continuously reoccur in their daily lives if they were to achieve. The same holds true today.

To undertake God's work without God's divine presence is to invite stagnation and defeat, whether it be in one's personal life, the local church, or the denomination. Polity, as important as it is, is in reality only a tool in the hands of dedicated and energized Christian workers. It must be kept in mind that organization, which takes its shape from polity, becomes somewhat like tools in the hands of a mechanic. The same principle holds with Christian workers who are given tools of organization and polity. Organization in and of itself is motionless and powerless. So is polity. The motivating force must come from above and in endless fashion for giant accomplishments to be realized. We may have a denomination of perfect organization, relationships, and procedures; however, nothing other than God's Spirit will energize us to make that organization function with force so that the mighty task at hand can be achieved. In this way God gets the glory, and we get the joy.

Dr. Truett had so wisely expressed it when he said that education is not to enable us to do less work but will help us accomplish vastly more with the same amount of effort. This is why submission to the Christian is so much more valuable than conquest. By yielding our all, we gain his might and power. If we spend our time as Baptists boasting that we have built the largest non-Catholic denomination in the nation, we are losing ground. If, however, we see that the gains realized have been through God's provisions of power and daily guidance we will continue to grow, and future generations of Baptists will accomplish far more than we have ever dreamed.

1845
Preamble and Constitution
of the
Southern Baptist Convention

We, the delegates from Missionary Societies, Churches, and other religious bodies of the Baptist Denomination, in various parts of the United States, met in Convention, in the city of Augusta, Georgia, for the purpose of carrying into effect the benevolent intentions of our constituents, by organizing a plan for eliciting, combining and directing the energies of the whole denomination in one sacred effort, for the propagation of the Gospel, agree to the following rules, or fundamental principles:

ARTICLE I. This body shall be styled the Southern Baptist Convention.

ARTICLE II. It shall be the design of this Convention to promote Foreign and Domestic Missions, and other important objects connected with the Redeemer's kingdom, and to combine for this purpose, such portions of the Baptist denomination in the United States, as may desire a general organization for Christian benevolence, which shall fully respect the independence and equal rights of the Churches.

ARTICLE III. A triennial Convention shall consist of members who contribute funds, or are delegated by religious bodies contributing funds, and the system of representation and terms of membership shall be as follows, viz: An annual contribution of one hundred dollars for three years next preceding the meeting, or the contribution of three hundred dollars at any time within said three years, shall entitle the contributor to one representative; an annual contribution of two hundred dollars, as aforesaid, shall entitle the contributor to two representatives; and so, for each additional one hundred dollars, an additional representative shall be allowed. Provided, however, that when application shall be made for the first time by bodies, or individuals, to be admitted into the Convention, one delegate shall be allowed for each one hundred dollars. And provided, also, that in case of great collateral Societies, composed of representatives, receiving contributions from different parts of the country, the ratio of representation shall be one delegate for every thousand dollars, annually contributed for three years, as aforesaid; but the number of representatives shall never exceed five.

ARTICLE IV. The officers of this Convention shall be a President, four Vice Presidents, a Treasurer, and two Secretaries, who shall be elected at each triennial meeting and hold their offices until a new election; and the officers of the Convention shall be, *each by virtue of his office*, members of the several Boards.

ARTICLE V. The Convention shall elect at each triennial meeting as many Boards of Managers, as in its judgment will be necessary for carrying out the benevolent objects it may determine to promote, all which Boards shall continue in office until a new election. Each Board shall consist of a President, Vice Presidents, Secretaries, Treasurer, Auditor, and fifteen other members, seven of whom, including one or more of the officers, shall form a quorum for the transaction of business. To each Board shall be committed, during the recess of the Convention, the entire management of all the affairs relating to the object with whose interest it shall be charged, all which management shall be in strict accordance with the constitutional provisions adopted by this Convention, and such other instructions as may be given from time to time. Each Board shall have power to make such compensation to its Secretaries and Treasurer, as it may think right; fill the vacancies occuring in its own body; enact its own by-laws; have an annual meeting at any place it may appoint, and other meetings at such times and places as it may think best; keep a record of its proceedings and present a report of them to the Convention at each triennial meeting.

ARTICLE VI. The Treasurer of each Board shall faithfully account for all monies received by him, keep a regular entry of all receipts and disbursements, and make report of them to the Convention, whenever it shall be in session, and to his Board as often as required. He shall also, on entering upon the duties of his office, give competent security to the President of his Board, for all the stock and funds committed to his care. His books shall be open at all times, to the inspection of any member of the Convention and of his Board. No monies shall be paid out of any of the Treasuries of the Boards, but by an order from that Board, from whose Treasury the money is to be drawn, which order shall be signed by its presiding officer.

ARTICLE VII. The Corresponding Secretaries of the several Boards shall maintain intercourse by letter, with such individuals or public bodies, as the interests of their respective bodies may require. Copies of all such communications, with their answers, if any, shall be kept by them on file.

ARTICLE VIII. The Recording Secretaries of the several Boards, shall keep a fair record of their proceedings, and of such other documents as may be committed to them for the purpose.

ARTICLE IX. All the Officers, Boards, Missionaries and Agents, appointed by the Convention, or by any of its Boards, shall be members of some regular Church, in union with the Churches composing this Convention.

ARTICLE X. Missionaries appointed by any of the Boards of this Convention, must, previous to their appointment, furnish evidence of genuine piety, fervent zeal in their Master's cause, and talents which fit them for the service for which they offer themselves.

ARTICLE XI. The bodies and individuals, composing this Convention, shall have the right to specify the object, or objects, to which their contributions shall be applied. But when no such specification is made, the Convention will make the appropriation at its own discretion.

ARTICLE XII. The Convention shall hold its meetings triennially, but extra meetings may be called by the President, with the approbation of any one of the Boards of Managers. A majority of the attending delegates, shall form a quorum for the transaction of business.

ARTICLE XIII. Any alterations which experience shall dictate, may be made in these articles, by a vote of two-thirds of the members present, at any triennial meeting of the Convention.

(From *Annual* of the Southern Baptist Convention, 1845, pp. 3-5.)

Address to the Public

It was a regular practice in 1845 to prepare an address to the public explaining the necessity and purpose of a new organization. The new Southern Baptist Convention followed this practice, and the speech was prepared by William B. Johnson.

THE SOUTHERN BAPTIST
CONVENTION,
To the Brethren in the United States;
to the congregations connected with
the respective Churches; and
to all candid men.

A painful division has taken place in the missionary operations of the American Baptists. We would explain the origin, the principles and the objects of that division, or the peculiar circumstances in which the organization of the Southern Baptist Convention became necessary.

Let not the extent of this disunion be exaggerated. At the present time it involves only the Foreign and Domestic Missions of the denomination. Northern and Southern Baptists are still brethren. They differ in no article of the faith. They are guided by the same principles of gospel order. Fanatical attempts have indeed been made, in some quarters, to exclude us of the South from Christian fellowship. We do not retort these attempts; and believe their extent to be comparatively limited. Our christian fellowship is not, as we feel, a matter to be obtruded on any one. We abide by that of our God, his dear Son, and all his baptized followers. The few ultra Northern brethren to whom we allude, must take what course they please. Their conduct has not influenced us in this movement. We do not regard the rupture as extending to foundation principles, nor can we think that the great body of our Northern brethren will so regard it. Disunion has proceeded, however, deplorably far. The first part of our duty is to show that its entire origin is with others. This is its history.

I. The General Convention of the Baptist denomination of the United States was composed of brethren from every part of the

American Republic. Its Constitution knows no difference between slaveholders and non-slaveholders. Nor during the period of its existence, for the last thirty years, has it, in practice, known any thing of this distinction. Both parties have contributed steadily and largely (if never adequately) to those funds which are the basis of its constituency; both have yielded its office-bearers of all grades; its missionaries and translators of God's word; its men of toils many, and of prayers not unavailing, abroad and at home. The honored dead of both these classes have walked in closest sympathy with each other; anticipating in the Board-room and in the Monthly Concert, that higher, but not holier union now in their case consummated. Throughout the entire management of its early affairs, the whole struggle with its early difficulties, there was no breath of discord between them. Its Richard Furman and its Wm. Staughton, its Jesse Mercer and its Thomas Baldwin, led on the sacramental host shoulder to shoulder, and heart to heart. Their rivalry being only in earnest efforts for a common cause, their entire aversions and enmities were directed with all the strength of their souls, against the common foe. And to the last, did they not cherish the strong belief that they left no other enmities or aversions; no other rivalry to their successors?

In particular, a special rule of the Constitution defines *who* may be missionaries, viz: "Such persons only as are in full communion with some church in our denomination; and who furnish satisfactory evidence of genuine piety, good talents, and fervent zeal for the Redeemer's cause." Now, while under this rule the slaveholder has been, in his turn, employed as a missionary, it is not alledged that any other persons than those above described, have been appointed. Moreover, the important post of a superintendent of the education of native missionaries, has been assigned, with universal approbation, to the pastor of one of our largest slaveholding churches.

But an evil hour arrived. Even our humble efforts in the conquest of the world to God, excited the accuser of our brethren to cast discord among us; and in the last two Triennial Conventions, slavery and anti-slavery men began to draw off on different sides. How did the nobler spirits on each side endeavor to meet this? They proposed and carried almost unanimously, the following explicit resolution:

"Resolved, That in co-operating together, as members of this Convention, in the work of foreign missions, we disclaim all sanction, either expressed or implied, whether of slavery or anti-slavery; but as individuals, we are free to express and to promote, elsewhere, our views on these subjects, in a christian manner and spirit."

Our successors will find it difficult to believe that so important and plain a declaration had become, before the close of the first year of the triennial period, a perfect nullity. In December last, the acting Board of the Convention, at Boston, adopted a new qualification for missionaries, a new special rule, viz: that "If any one who shall offer himself for a missionary, having slaves, should insist on retaining them as his property, they could not appoint him." "One thing is certain," they continue, "we could never be a party to any arrangement which implies approbation of slavery."

We pray our brethren and all candid men to mark the date of this novel rule—the close of the first six months of their three years' power, a date at which the compromise resolution could scarcely have reached our remoter mission stations. If usurpation had been intended, could it have been more fitly timed? An usurpation of ecclesiastical power quite foreign to our polity. Such power was assumed at a period when the aggrieved "thousands of Israel" had, as it now appears, no practical remedy. Its obvious tendency was, either our final subjugation to that power, or a serious interruption of the flow of Southern benevolence. The latter was the far more probable evil; and the Boston Board knew this well. They were from various quarters apprised of it. We, on the other hand, did not move in the matter of a new organization until three liberal States had refused to send northward any more contributions. Our leaders had chosen new rules. Thus came war within our gates: while the means of war on the common enemy were daily diminishing.

By this decision, the Board had placed itself in direct opposition to the Constitution of the Convention. The only reason given for this extraordinary and unconstitutional dictum being—that "The appointing power for wise and good purposes, is confided to the acting Board." On such a slight show of authority, this Board undertook to declare that to be a disqualification in one who should offer himself for a missionary, which the Convention had said shall *not* be a disqualification. It had also expressly given its sanction to anti-slavery opinions, and impliedly fixed its condemnation on slavery, although the Convention had said that "neither" should be done. And further, it forbade those who shall apply for a missionary appointment, to "express and promote elsewhere" their views on the subject of slavery in a right "manner and spirit," when the Convention declared they "were free" to do so. These brethren, thus acted upon a sentiment they have failed to prove—That slavery is, in all circumstances, sinful. Whereas their own solemn resolution in the last Convention, (their's as much as our's) left us free to promote slavery. Was not this leaving us free, and *"in a Christian spirit and manner"* to promote that which in their hearts, and according to the present shewing of their conduct, they regard as a sin?

Enough, perhaps, has been said of the origin of this movement. Were we asked to characterize the conduct of our Northern brethren in one short phrase, we should adopt that of the Apostle. It was "FORBIDDING US *to speak* UNTO THE GENTILES." Did this deny us no privilege? Did it not obstruct us, lay a kind of Romish interdict upon us in the discharge of an imperative duty; a duty to which the church has been, after the lapse of ages, awakened universally and successfully; a duty the very object, and only object, of our long cherished connection and confederation?

And this would seem the place to state, that our Northern brethren were dealt with as brethren to the last moment. Several of our churches cherished the hope that by means of remonstrance and expostulation, through the last Annual Meeting of the Board of Managers, at Providence, the Acting Board might be brought to feel the grievous wrong they had inflicted. The Managing Board was therefore affectionately and respectfully addressed on the subject, and was entreated to revise and reverse the obnoxious interdict. Alas! the results were—contemptuous silence as to the application made; and a deliberate resolve, expressing sympathy with the Acting Board, and a determination to sustain them.

II. THE PRINCIPLES of the Southern Baptist Convention, it remains then to be stated, are conservative; while they are also, as we trust, equitable and liberal. They propose to do the Lord's work in the way our fathers did it. Its title designates at once its origin, and the simple, firm abiding of the South on the ground from which it has been so unconstitutionally and unjustly attempted to eject us. We have but enquired for "the old paths" of missionary operations; "asked" for, and attempted to restore the practically "good way." The Constitution we adopt is precisely that of the original union; that in connection with which throughout his missionary life, Adoniram Judson has lived, and under which Ann Judson and Boardman have died. We recede from it no single step. We have constructed for our basis no new creed; acting in this matter upon a Baptist aversion for all creeds but the Bible. We use the very terms, as we uphold the true spirit and great object of the late "General Convention of the Baptist denomination of the United States." It is they who wrong us that have receded. We have receded neither from the Constitution nor from any part of the original ground on which we met them in this work, And if, we ask in parting, the original and broad Bible ground of confederation were not equitable, how came it so nobly and so long to be acted upon? If equitable, why depart from it?

We claim to have acted in the premises, with liberality towards our Northern brethren. Thrust from the common platform of equal rights, between the Northern and Southern churches, we have but reconstructed that platform. Content with it, we adhere to it, and reproduce it, as broad enough for us and for them. Have they thrust us off? We retain but one feeling in the case. *That we will not practically leave it on any account:* much less in obedience to such usurped authority, or in deference to such a manifest breach of trust as is here involved. A breach of covenant that looks various ways—heavenward and earthward. For we repeat, THEY WOULD FORBID US TO *speak unto* THE GENTILES. The Jerusalem church, then, must be regathered at the suspected Samaria, or at some new centre of operations, like Antioch. "One thing is certain"—We must go every where preaching the word.—"We can never be a party to any arrangement" for monopolizing the Gospel: any arrangement which like that of the Autocratical Interdict of the North, would first drive us from our beloved colored people, of whom they prove that they know nothing comparatively, and from the much-wronged Aborigines of the country;—and then cut us off from the whitening fields of the heathen harvest-labor; to which by cogent appeals and solemn prayers, they have so often protested that, without us, they were inadequate.

III. OUR OBJECTS, then, are the extension of the Messiah's kingdom, and the glory of our God. Not disunion with any of his people; not the upholding of any form of human policy, or civil rights; but God's glory, and Messiah's increasing reign; in the promotion of which, we find no necessity for relinquishing any of our civil rights. We will never interfere with *what is Caesar's*. We will not compromit what is God's.

These objects will appear in detail on the face of our Constitution, and in the proceedings, which accompany this address. They are distributed, at present, between two acting Boards for Foreign and Domestic Missions, having their respective seats at Richmond, Va., and Marion, Ala. We sympathise with the Macedonian cry from every part of the heathen world,—with the low moan, for spiritual aid, of the four millions of half stifled Red Men, our neighbors; with the sons of Ethiopia among us, stretching forth their hands of supplication for the gospel, to God and all his people,—and we have shaken ourselves from the night mare of a six years' "strife about words to *no* profit," for the profit of these poor, perishing and precious souls. Our language to all America, and to all christendom, if they will hear us, is *"come over,"* and for *these* objects, as ye love souls, and the divine Saviour of souls, *"help us."* We ask help at this juncture for nothing else. We have had more talk than work about these objects too long. We have waited quite too long for the more learned and gifted, and opulent, and worthy, to lead our way toward these objects; and we have shortened debate upon them to get to business. Our eyes and hearts are turned with feelings of parental fondness to Burmah and the Karens; with a zeal in which we are willing to be counselled by God and all considerate men, (but by none else,) to the continent of Africa, and her pernicious fountains of idolatry, oppression and blood; but yet more, with unutterable hope and thankfulness, to China and her providentially opened ports, and teeming thirsty millions. Among us, in the South, we have property, which we will offer to the Lord and his cause, in these channels—some prudence with which we would have our best wisdom to dwell; and professions of a piety which we seek to have increased and purified, like that of the first Baptist churches, when they had "rest; and walking in the fear of the Lord, and in the comfort of the Holy Ghost, were multiplied."

In parting with beloved brethren and old co-adjustors in this cause, we could weep, and have wept, for ourselves and for them; but the season, as well of weeping as of vain jangling, is, we are constrained to believe, just now past. For years the pressure of men's hands has been upon us far too heavily. Our brethren have pressed upon every inch of our privileges and our sacred rights— but this shall only urge our gushing souls to yield proportionately of their renewed efforts to the Lord, to the church universal, and to a dying world; even as water pressed from without rises but the more within. Above all, the mountain pressure of our obligations to God, even our own God; to Christ and to Him crucified; and to the personal and social blessings of the Holy Spirit and his influences, shall urge our little streams of the water of life to flow forth; until every wilderness and desolate place within our reach (and what extent of the world's wilderness wisely considered is not within our reach?) "shall be glad"—even at this passing calamity of division; and the deserts of unconverted human nature "rejoice and blossom as the rose."

By order of the Convention.

WILLIAM B. JOHNSON, D.D.

Augusta, Ga., 12th May, 1845.
    (*Ibid.*, pp. 17-20.)

The First Charter

Act of Incorporation

Be it enacted by the Senate and House of Representatives of the State of Georgia, in General Assembly, met, and it is hereby enacted by the authority of the same, That William B. Johnson, Wilson Lumpkin, James B. Taylor, A. Dockery, R. B. C. Howell, and others, their associates and successors, be, and they are hereby, incorporated and made a body politic, by the name and style of the "Southern Baptist Convention," with authority to receive, hold, possess, retain and dispose of property, either real or personal, to sue and be sued, and to make all by-laws, rules and regulations necessary to the transaction of their business, not inconsistent with the laws of this State, or of the United States: Said corporation being created for the purpose of eliciting, combining and directing the energies of the Baptist denomination of christians, for the propagation of the gospel, any law, usage or custom to the contrary notwithstanding.

Approved, December 27th, 1845.

(From *Annual* of the Southern Baptist Convention, 1846, p. 37.)

All of the materials quoted above are reprinted from A Baptist Source Book, *by Robert A. Baker, Broadman Press © 1966.*